*The Kabbalistic Tree of Life*

By the same author:

Adam and The Kabbalistic Trees
A Kabbalistic Universe
The Way of Kabbalah
Introduction to the World of Kabbalah
The Kabbalist at Work
Kabbalah and Exodus
School of the Soul
Psychology and Kabbalah
Kabbalah and Astrology
The Anointed–*a Kabbalistic novel*
The Anatomy of Fate
The Path of a Kabbalist
A Kabbalistic View of History

By Other Publishers:

Kabbalah—The Divine Plan (HarperCollins)
Kabbalah, Tradition of Hidden Knowledge (Thames & Hudson)
Astrology, The Celestial Mirror (Thames & Hudson)
As Above So Below (Stuart & Watkins)

*The Kabbalistic Tree of Life*
*Z'ev ben Shimon Halevi*

**Kabbalah
Society**

Bet El Trust
Registered Charity No. 288712

www.kabbalahsociety.org
E-mail: books@kabbalahsociety.org

First published in 1972 by Rider & Co.
Revised Edition in 2009 by Kabbalah Society
Copyright © Z'ev ben Shimon Halevi 1972, 2009

*The illustrations on Pages 61 and 113 are reproduced by kind
permission of Dover Publications Inc.*

A CIP catalogue record for this book
is available from the British Library.

ISBN: 978-1-909171-12-1

Printed and bound by Lightning Source UK Ltd., Milton Keynes

Design by Tree of Life Publishing
www.treeoflifepublishing.co.uk

For Glyn Davies
A Kabbalistic Merlin

# *Acknowledgements*

I would like to thank every person who, consciously or unconsciously, living or dead, has contributed to this work. Particularly, I am grateful to my forefathers and to various personal mentors, especially those in the tradition of the Society of the Common Life.

# *Contents*

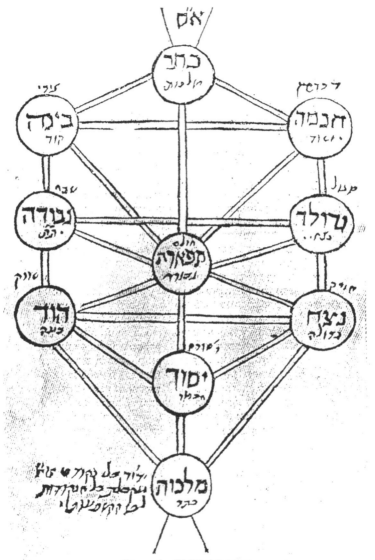

*Figure 1—TREE OF LIFE*
*This diagram is at the heart of Kabbalah. It is a kind of mandala that embodies the*
*symbols and metaphysics of Existence. The ten circles represent the Divine principles*
*that govern all that is manifest while the twenty-two paths define their relationship to*
*each other. The triads are the areas in which the dynamic and structure of the Tree*
*and God's Will come into play. This image first appeared in the public domain in the*
*Middle Ages.* (Moses Cordovero, 16th century).

# *Illustrations*

# *Preface to the Revised Edition*

*Tree of Life, An Introduction to the Cabala*, as this book was previously titled, was written nearly forty years ago. Much has been learned since then. In this revised edition, I have cut out some chapters and added new material that expands the Tree of Life diagram's full significance.

The kabbalistic Tree of Life is a metaphysical symbol based upon the Menorah, the seven-branched Candlestick described in the Bible. Moses was given the design on Mount Sinai, in a revelation along with the Ten Commandments. It is the archetypal model of the Laws of Existence and has been used by Kabbalists over the millennia as an object of contemplation. It explains the dynamic, structure and purpose of the Universe. This book sets out to demonstrate how its principles apply not only to the Cosmos in its fullness but any distinct entity within it, especially human beings, who are a microcosmic image of God. The Laws embodied in the Tree manifest in many ways from the mundane to the sacred. When seen in its totality, what is called the Great Tree becomes the basis of the Chain of Being, known in Kabbalah as Jacob's Ladder.

Z'ev ben Shimon Halevi
London
Spring 2009/5769

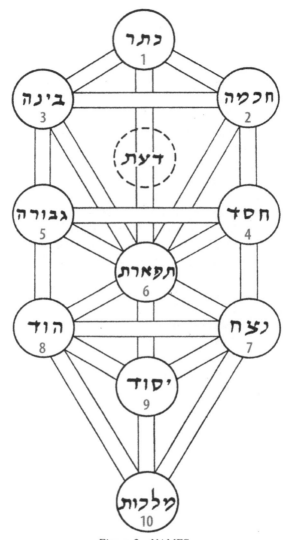

*Figure 2—NAMES*

*Here the sefirot or Numbers one to ten, also seen as Sapphires, Vessels and the Hands of God, are given names from the Bible. These vary according to different Kabbalistic schools. They all, however, represent the same particular Divine attributes, qualities or functions. As such they are not the Godhead but expressions of the Absolute. These names are the Hebrew words of a Divine song but not the Singer. The world will exist as long as the melody is sung and then, at the end of Time, vanish into the silence of Nothingness from whence it came. The dotted circle was added later as the unmanifest aspect of the Tree.* (Calligraphy by Gila Davis).

# Introduction

The Tree of Life is a picture of Creation. It is an objective diagram of the principles working throughout the Universe. Cast in the form of an analogic Tree it demonstrates the flow of forces down from the Divine to the lowest World and back again. In it are contained all the laws that govern Existence and their interaction. It is also a comprehensive view of man.

The relative Universe hovers between two poles, All and Nothing. Either end of this fluctuating axis may be seen as Nothing or All as both become the entry and exit points for the Absolute who stands apart from Creation. Here we have the full reality. All else is, to the ultimate observer, illusion — a cosmic drama composed and dissolved in a cyclic round of plays within plays from the subtlest reverberations in the highest Worlds to the slowest movements and changes in the coarsest Materiality.

The Absolute has no direct contact with Creation yet it permeates through the matrix of the Universe, supporting it like the silence behind every sound. Without this negative reality nothing could come into existence, as shadow cannot manifest without light. Here, in the relative world, we move amid particles and waves never suspecting that what we touch is always disappearing and what we see is not really there. Solidity is a charade, a temporary state of nothing, frozen for a time into a form that is familiar to us who are ourselves but travellers in the ever changing scenery called Earth.

Creation is separate from its Creator, even more than a modern production of Hamlet is far removed from Shakespeare. Yet Creation bears its Author's hand and, though the actors may interpret, the play remains essentially as the Master conceived it. The relative Universe, like our analogy of a play, is constructed in the same design with protagonists and supporting cast set against a series of backgrounds in which different rôles, seeking to find equilibrium, create and operate dramatic events known as evolution.

The relationships between the various actors or forces is very precise, though they may take up different attitudes under specific

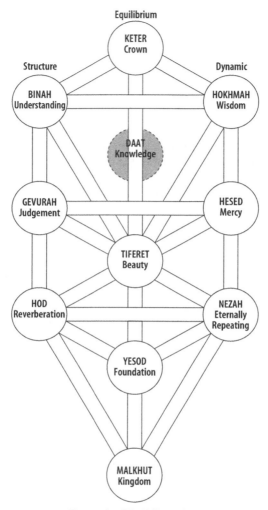

*Figure 3—TRANSLATION.*
*Beneath each name is the equivalent in English. However, a Hebrew root word can have several meanings. Hokhmah can be seen as Revelation and Binah, Reason. Likewise, Hesed and Gevurah can be said to represent Charity and Severity; while Nezah can be seen as endless repetition instead of Victory, as commonly translated. Hod or Glory, as it is sometimes called, comes from the idea of the shimmering vibration of a peacock's tail. The Crown and the Kingdom are clearly Ruler and Ruled while the non-sefirah, Knowledge, refers to direct experience. The name Beauty is given because it is at the central focus of the Tree and Foundation, again a nominal title, is about the image of things embodied in the substance of Malkhut. (Halevi).*

conditions. This set of combinations is laid out in the Tree of Life so that a given situation may be examined and its participants and their true status can be revealed.

The Tree is a model of the relative Universe. It is the template of all the Worlds, carrying within it a recurring system of order. Moreover, any complete organism or organisation is an imitation of its plan. Man is the prime example. He is a microcosm of the macrocosm. His being is an exact replica in every detail in miniature of the cosmoses above him. True, he moves in the physical World, is made up of atoms, molecules and cells yet he partakes in the subtle realm of Forms, can assist in conscious Creation and has access to the Divine.

As man is an image of Creation so Creation is but a reflection of the Creator. By this resemblance we are able to study that which is below by looking at that which is above and that which we cannot observe above by examining that which is below. Through the Tree of Life we have an objective connection which gives us insight and knowledge by the principle of parallel—into the upper and lower, inner and outer Universes.

In our account the origin of the Tree of Life is traced, then the power of its illumination and formulation. Following the development of its conception we see that cosmic principles apply to any whole entity. Observing its workings we are shown how the Tree gathers into an intelligible order all aspects of phenomena and demonstrates them in a reflective picture, a Universe wherein the Creator is present even in the densest of matter.

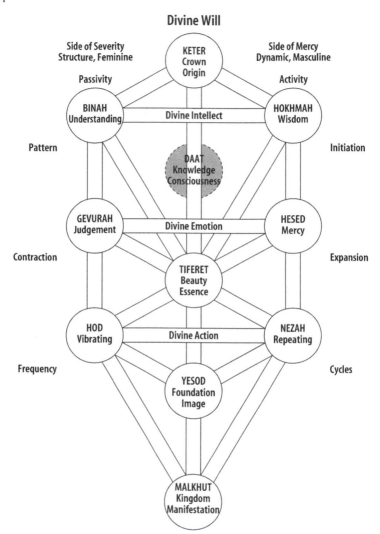

*Figure 4—METAPHYSICS*
*In this Tree, the functions of the Tree are set out in philosophical and scientific terms.*
*The Crown is clearly where the whole process of Manifestation begins. Initiation is*
*followed by the pattern to be followed, like conception gives rise to an embryo of a*
*particular species. The functions of expansion and contraction balance off any*
*excesses while the cycles and their frequencies govern the rhythms of the universe.*
*There these three pairs also define the three levels of Divine intellect, emotion and*
*action while the central column marks out the degrees of consciousness to be found*
*in this image of God. (Halevi).*

# 1. History

The actual origin of the Tree of Life is unknown. It is traditionally rooted in the Kabbalah, the inner teaching of Judaism. All complete religions have two faces. The outer facet takes the form of words and public ritual while the inner aspect is the internal, often an oral instruction which is passed on from teacher to pupil who, face-to-face, have a personal rapport in which the Master knows what and when can be taught to further the disciple's development. When the pupil becomes a master in his own right he, in turn, imparts his own wisdom and understanding to the next generation, so that without a break a Tradition may be carried on over several thousand years, with no trace of its outward appearance.

This oral method is common to all the major religions. However, like many human institutions it is subject to decay and corruption so that from time to time in history there is a reformulation of ancient objective principles adapted for the language and customs of the current day.

It is said that Abraham, the father of the Hebrew nation, received the original Teaching from Melchizedek, King of Salem, who was also a priest of the most high God. The name Melchizedek means 'King of just men' or 'my King is righteousness' and Salem, the ancient name for Jerusalem, means 'peace'. This may be seen as historical fact or allegory, for the Bible can be read as an outer or inner account of events which take on the form of living parables.

Prior to this happening, Abraham had come to the conclusion, after deep research in contemporary religions, that there was only one, invisible, living God. Now, after being initiated by Melchizedek, matched to this belief was the introduction to objective knowledge, an understanding that out of the creative fountainhead of God came many manifestations and that these were not to be mistaken for the Creator. Abraham, knowing that he was known by God, made a pact with Him to pass the knowledge on. This was the Covenant.

The Hebrews retained this understanding with their Maker over many generations, though occasionally they lost sight of it when their

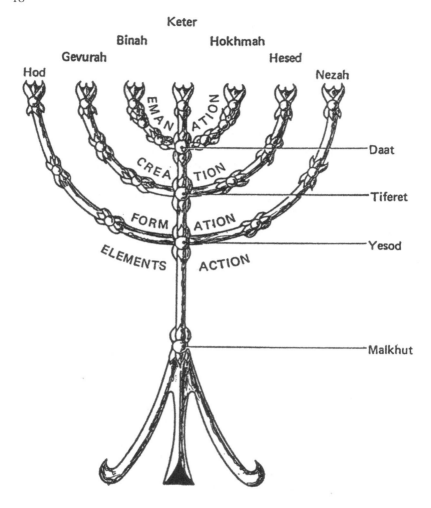

*Figure 5—MENORAH*

*This is the original Tree of Life. Its design was given to Moses on Mount Sinai. It was made of a single piece of gold, the Divine metal, representing the unity of Existence. It has two wings and a central pillar. Those represent the three principles that underlie Existence like the Yang, Yin and Dao of the Chinese esoteric tradition. There are seven candle holders with the Crown at the centre of the six side-pillar sefirot. The middle column has four junctions, representing the central sefirot, with the twenty-two decorations setting out the paths. The spaces in between the arms indicate the four Worlds which will emerge from this primordial image of the Divine Realm.* (Halevi).

tradition was adulterated by neighbouring customs and beliefs. The essence, however, was periodically revived as when Moses dragged a half-reluctant slave-minded people out of the symbolic, as well as literal, land of Egypt into a spiritual rebirth. In the desert of Sinai a whole generation of old slave habits had to die off before a new Israel could be set on its original direction.

Without doubt objective knowledge about the Universe was held at the time of Solomon for it is written into the biblical text of the period. The construction of the Temple and the seven-branched candlestick are both formulations of the Tree of Life, as were the columns Jachin and Boaz on either side of the Temple veil. The physical diagram of the Tree built into the Temple was lost when this first Temple was destroyed and the Jews were taken into exile in Babylon.

In Babylon strange events occurred. Besides Ezekiel's resurrection of Israel's religious tradition, which urged them to return home to Jerusalem, the men responsible for the inner teaching of the religion realised that here was a unique possibility at the second rebirth of the nation. Hebrew, in the over-riding presence of the vernacular used in Babylonia, had ceased to be a first language. So here was a chance to embed, before it became established again as a national speech, many ideas—make it a language that contained more than just an everyday vocabulary of meanings. At this point we know that the actual twenty-two letters of the alphabet were reconstructed, changed from the ancient pictograms into a more robust alphabet known as the Syrian script.

Later, long after this new Hebrew had been established, (though it never quite took over from Aramaic, the *lingua franca* of the Middle East), it became regarded as a holy language and, like Sanskrit, to be used in holy matters.

One work in particular reveals the philosophical construction of the Hebrew alphabet. This was the *Sefer Yezirah*, reputed to be written by Abraham but more likely to have been drafted in the earlier centuries of the common era. In this to each letter was ascribed a planet and a Sign of the Zodiac. Herein lies our date clue in as much that the Sign Libra was inserted into the Zodiac circle long after Abraham died. Other qualities were attached to each letter and the whole pivoted on a system of the three creative principles embodied in Air, Water and Fire. Here the various combinations of these three forces made the Universe function and numerous arrangements of letters and their corresponding numerical values described the positions and relationships

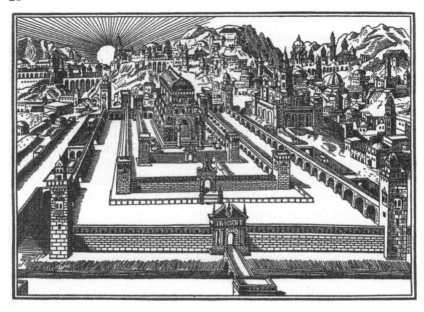

*Figure 6—TEMPLE*

*This is an idealised picture of Solomon's Temple. Even so, it contains in its imagery the kabbalistic scheme of Existence. The lowest level is the courtyard of Gentiles. Then there is the outer court, representing the physical World, with the inner court defining the World of Formation. The Sanctuary, with its two pillars, symbolises the dimension of Creation while the unseen Holy of Holies within signifies the Divine realm. The three gates hold the central axis of the middle column of Grace. The social strata of Israelites, Levites, priests and high priests represent the four levels within the microcosm of humanity. (Passover Haggadah, 17th century).*

evident in the macrocosm of the world and the microcosm of man. Drawing possibly from Greek sources it also used the Pythagorean concepts of a triangle or trinity containing the ten letters relating to the name of God. Scholars disagree as to who formulated this diagram first.

The interchange of objective knowledge between wise men of different nations and traditions during the few hundred years before Christ was more common than is generally supposed. Intelligent men obviously met and exchanged ideas while their fellows fought over trade and politics. The Jews, though often considered a particularly insular group, were no exception as far as the perceptive thinkers amongst them were concerned. While Pythagoras travelled the Eastern Mediterranean in search of knowledge, no doubt rabbis, though not of the merely learned kind, also sought wise company — even in alien cultures. In the seaport of Alexandria, founded by the Greeks, a great library devoted to the nine Muses was set up. Here at this first museum were gathered ideas from all over the known world. To this remarkable centre, one of the early Ptolemies invited seventy Jews so that the Hebrew books of which he had heard respectful reports might be translated into Greek. With these scholars no doubt came rabbis versed in Kabbalah, the inner explanation of the Bible. These men probably made connections with the inner teachings of Greek and Egyptian philosophy and religion and from this cross pollination more discoveries were added to the distinct traditions. There is much evidence of shared ideas in Greek thought and an uncheckable fable has it that the Tarot cards, which appear in Renaissance times, trace back to the wall diagrams in the corridors of Egyptian temples. These cards, on close scrutiny, show more Greek and Hebraic thinking than Egyptian symbolism.

The adding of new ideas and reformulating of old ones was a feature of the Kabbalah Schools and rabbis down the centuries have hammered and tested every addition before its inclusion into the body of kabbalistic literature. The test of argument, along with the flash of enlightenment, kept a balance necessary for the narrow path of vision through the forest of illusion. For this reason men were not allowed to study the Kabbalah until their full maturity, lest the wine of mysticism overbalanced them like a drug trip of the modern young. A man had to be experienced in life, have the stability to handle and master the things of Earth before he could attempt the portals of Heaven.

It is said by some scholars that the first writings on Kabbalah were

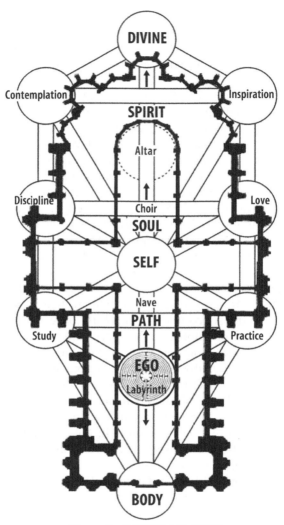

*Figure 7—CATHEDRAL TREE*
*This is the ground plan of Chartres, built in the Middle Ages. The discovery that the geometry of the Tree fitted exactly into the design is startling until the history of this first formal school in Western Christendom reveals that the Jewish quarter was just across the street from the site. Moreover, it is known that the Stone Masons' guild that specialised in building sacred structures practised their own spirituality. This is indicated by the labyrinth, the symbol that represents the ordinary ego mind circling round until it discovers the way out and up to the Self and beyond. There must have been some collusion with the clergy of Chartres who clearly were acquainted with esoteric ideas.* (Discovered by Prof. Keith Critchlow).

set down in the second century of the common era by people present at the discussions of Rabbi Simeon ben Yohai. It is maintained by other scholars that many, if not all, of the books of the *Zohar* commentaries were written or compiled by a twelfth-century Spanish Jew, Moses de Leon, whose widow claimed he wrote them to make money under the blind of their being ancient works because people then, as now, like and value antiques. This does not matter. More important was that the Kabbalah emerged into the open and we get in medieval Spain, which took over from the decaying authority of the Babylonian rabbinical school, the full diagram of the Tree of Life.

Besides its effect on the golden Arab-Jewish era in Spain, Kabbalah and its ideas had a powerful influence on Christendom. The Church was, at that point, in need of reassurance for its more intelligent clergy who were being disturbed by the quality of ideas coming from Muslim and Jewish universities and were consequently finding that Faith was not enough. Helped by others Thomas Aquinas, the Catholic scholar, found the solution in his study of Judaism which combined the kabbalistic work of Dionysius the Areopagite with that of Aristotle. Out of this he was able to formulate a whole theology which was later to be grafted into Church teaching. Contrary to the platonic Christians he brought the abstract universe into the mundane, relating God and angelic influences through the Tree of Life to the world of elements, plants, animals and men. Out of this kabbalistic concept came the nine orders of the Church hierarchy. Even the great cathedral builders were influenced. Erected by the Masons, who based their ideas on the Temple of Solomon, the West front of each church had two towers representing the twin columns on either side of the Temple veil. Here were the two outer columns of the Tree of Life, the masculine and feminine aspects, the active and passive forces, flowing down from Heaven. Called, in Chartres cathedral, the Sun and Moon towers, this idea is repeated in later centuries though the source reason is forgotten. Another concept is the Holy Trinity of Father, Son and Holy Ghost with the kabbalistic Bride represented in the rose window of submission. Looked at with a knowing eye, many cathedral plans take on a new meaning.

By Renaissance times Kabbalah and the Tree of Life were known to many scholars. The *Zohar*, with its complex of studies on the Bible, numerology, angels, the nature of man and many other allied subjects, had been printed and Gentile scholars took much interest, partly to relate it with the knowledge coming in from the Byzantine world and

24

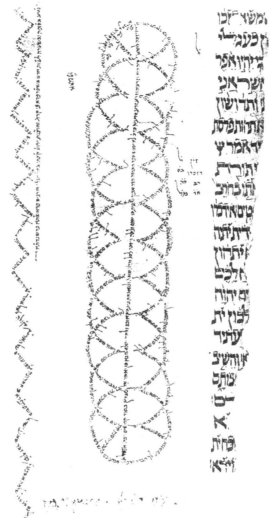

*Figure 8—COSMIC LADDER*

*The Jewish community was spread, during the Middle Ages, all over the known world. As non-Christians and non-Muslims, they could travel freely almost anywhere as merchants along the trade routes, East and West. Besides dealing with spices, precious stones and other rare commodities, they carried letters, books and ideas. Here, from a letter, is a Kabbalistic diagram composed of Biblical texts. It is an incomplete version of what was to become known as Jacob's Ladder. The sefirot and paths that interlock the four Worlds are left out because it might confuse those who had no metaphysical background. This is why the sefirotic Tree was kept secret until medieval times.* (Manuscript from the Yemeni School).

partly because of its relationship with magic. This application of Kabbalah brought it into much disrepute, even among the Jews themselves, for it gave rise to occasional mass psychosis and outlandish movements in certain northern European Jewish communities who desperately needed some mystical straw to hang on to during the recurrent waves of persecution.

This magical side, mostly misunderstood or fractionally digested, both fascinated and repulsed men who came in contact with Kabbalah. To the genuine scholar and philosopher it was a Jacob's Ladder up to Heaven, a method of study, the basis of a righteous code and a point of reference upon which to relate contemporary art and science. To the charlatan and the aspiring professional guru it was a magical weapon to cajole, frighten and fascinate individuals and groups. Like twentieth century technology, it could be made to work for or against man, lifting him out of the mire of drudgery or destroying his soul and body. At one end of the scale Kabbalists discussed the nature of the Universe with Pico della Mirandola, brilliant light of the Medici court; at the other end kabbalistic amulets were sold to keep off evil spirits or injure enemies. Popular Kabbalah reached its height in the seventeenth and eighteenth centuries with several false Messiahs all of whom, except one, disappointing their followers. This one saint, Israel Baal Shem, a natural mystic, was the focus of the Jewish revival movement called the Hassidim who flourish to this day. However, much of this Kabbalah was based on visions and wonder working and, while Judaism received a much needed impetus, the movement was more related to the parallel revivalism then going on in Christendom than to philosophy. Hassidism thrived, though not without resistance from the orthodox rabbis, even to the point of Baal Shem's excommunication. In time this great thrust of energy lost force and became formalised and institutionalised by custom rather than by spontaneous conviction. However, the so-called kabbalistic practices still continued, so that even amongst the nineteenth century Jewish immigrants from eastern Europe to the West there were to be found Kabbalists who would make charms to offset the evil eye.

This degeneracy of outer Kabbalah did not, however, hinder the researches of thoughtful Jews and Gentiles. Work was still carried out wherever Kabbalah and the Tree of Life were intelligently considered. Most of this effort was of scholarship, a blend of the intellectual detective with a dash of hope that some key might unlock the mystery. Many books were written and ideas developed but none of the quality

26

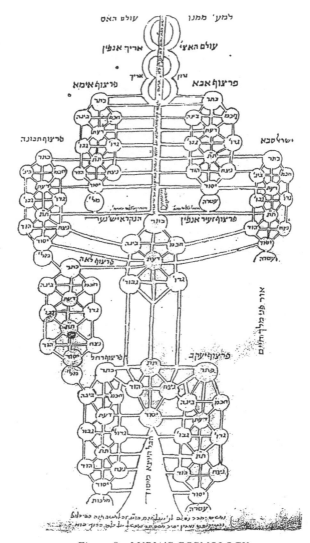

*Figure 9—LURIA'S COSMOLOGY*
*Isaac Luria formed his own school of Kabbalah in 16th century Safed, a hill town in Israel. He broke with the integrated view of Existence that traditional Kabbalah held by inventing his own system. In this, the Ladder of Worlds was shattered by the breaking up of this primordial Tree of Life because of the overwhelming power of the Divine influx coming from the Absolute. This was Luria's explanation for evil. However, even though this event is not mentioned in the Book of Genesis, which said that Creation was 'Tov Meod'—Very Good—Lurianic Kabbalah took over the traditional view because it seemed to explain history.* (19th century Lurianic scroll).

of the Middle Ages and earlier. The seventeeth century produced many speculative contributions but by the nineteenth century the natural sciences had begun to interest thinkers more than mysticism.

In the nineteenth century in the West various semi-religious movements, composed of people disappointed in materialism and their own formal religion, arose. These groups also included Jews who felt that orthodox Judaism did not fulfil their philosophical needs. Rabbinical discussion had become mere learnèd argument. There was no longer spontaneous wisdom and understanding or real interest in the inner meaning of Judaism, especially when Jewish intelligence became involved with the concept of Zionism.

Gradually the objective of Jerusalem shifted from the spiritual to the practical and politics took over from polemics. Zion, the yearned-for home of the exile, changed from man's seeking to regain Eden into the reinstatement of a nation in Palestine.

At the present time Judaism, like all formal religions, is losing its hold on the younger generation. However, this does not mean our time is irreligious. Far from it. Many of the young are seriously looking for meaning in a complex and conflicting world situation. Many people are at this moment involved in seeking out the truth through drugs and others belong to esoteric groups studying numerous systems and methods. Many of these organisations are based on the Oriental approach and are sometimes quite alien to the Western temperament. While it is argued that these give a fresh outlook, the effects of this adulteration occasionally divide a man, creating spiritual conflict. One cannot mix traditions and cultural temperament so easily. Every philosophy and religion is peculiar to its own place; moreover the English hippy in Kathmandu is not only half way between East and West but also ancient and modern times. Here lies a dangerous limbo so often entered by quite sincere people. In the West we have our own traditions, just as old as the East and as well tried. Kabbalah is one of them and an integral part of the Judaic-Greco-Christian tradition of Europe.

This then is our brief. The Tree of Life, as the name implies, is concerned with the living word. It exists now, in the twenty-first century, as well as in eternity. Our task is to transcribe the Tree into modern idiom so that it becomes manifest for us and others. Unless the top sefirah of Keter is connected with the bottom sefirah of Malkhut the Tree of Life is incomplete—and Heaven cannot reach Earth.

# 2. *Negative Existence*

There is an Absolute and a relative Universe. Between them lie the veils of negative existence. The Absolute is beyond even eternity. It is timeless, without form, without substance—beyond existence. It is nothing and everything. It undergoes no change yet is not changeless— it just is.

The relative Universe is the manifestation of Creation, the unfolding of a divine impulse, a vast seedbed coming into flower, then fruit which on completion decays, dies, and returns to its source ready to be born again.

Within this huge complex everything has its time and place and though some features and functions appear on vastly different scales of size and lifespan every one fits precisely into a whole, as our Sun fits into the scheme of the Milky Way and a liver cell relates to our body. Superficially the substances of the Universe may appear to be similar but the water of the sea, for instance, is not the same as that of a pond, nor can it support the same kinds of life. It is the relative position that alters its function. Moreover a molecule of water, continuing the example, may pass through many states. First as vapour such a molecule may be buffeted in a cloud. Then after falling within a drop locked on to a nucleus of dust, it becomes one of millions in a puddle that seeps into the earth, before being absorbed by a plant. For a time it may be fixed in the organic structure, part of the juices which, in turn, are sucked out of the plant fibres by an animal. There it flows in the blood stream of the creature until perhaps that animal is killed and eaten by man. Here again the molecule passes through many diverse experiences in the human body until it is excreted. Having got this far it passes through the various mechanical, chemical and organic processes of a sewage works before being released into a river where it flows with a myriad other molecules of water, all with quite different tales to tell, back to the sea. There it might spend several centuries in the depths before being convected up to the surface and evaporated into the atmosphere as cloud again. This is the relative world in miniature.

*Figure 10—ORIGINS*

*The medieval Kabbalists explained the origin of Existence in metaphysical terms. They defined God as Ayin, Absolute No-Thing, and En Sof, Absolute All or the limit-less. In order for God to behold God, the Mirror of Existence had to be brought into being. This required a space to be generated by the Absolute withdrawing to allow a space to appear. Here the three words at the top are Ayin and En Sof. Below is a ring of fire, symbolising the Will of the Absolute, within which is the Void of Negative Existence. Into this hollow were emanated the ten sefirot that govern relative Existence. In this way, the Kabbalists defined the beginning of the relative Universe and all its grades.* (Graphic by James Russell, 20th century).

In the relative Universe it is a question of time and position. The Sun is middle-aged in comparison to most stars and the Earth is still adolescent with its first growth of green hair on its face. Mankind, by its general performance, is probably in its childhood—judging by its periodic tantrums and breaking of toys! All is relative, each level fitting into the one above and containing the one below, the whole fitting into a grand design from the highest and most potent energy down to the densest of elements. Here we have the top of the Tree of Life, Keter the Crown and the bottom, Malkhut the Kingdom.

The Tree of Life defines the relative Universe at all levels. It is the archetypal pattern. However, above it, beyond Keter—the Hollow Crown through which the Creator manifests—lies the unmanifest of negative existence.

Negative existence is the intermediary zone between the Godhead and Creation. It is the pause before the music begins, the silence behind each note, the blank canvas beneath every painting and the empty space ready to be filled. Without this void nothing could have its being. It is a void, yet without it and its potential the relative Universe could not come into manifestation.

Negative existence is ever-present on all levels of Creation. It lies behind space and time. Without it there could be no galaxies or men. It contains—as a room's space does—the void in which we live. Emptiness is the still background against which time moves. Negative existence enables a man to be what he is. Mirror of Mirrors, negative existence's non-interference allows the most perfect reflection of Creation.

The veil nearest to the relative Universe is En Sof Aur—the Limitless Light—that is, that which is everywhere and penetrates even the thickest matter, as do certain cosmic rays which are so fine they pass clean through our planet as physical light does through a pane of glass.

The second veil of which we know even less is En Sof—the Limitless. This is the first step towards manifestation of the Creator. It is the point where Ayin the Ultimate void begins to focus out of Nothing into the Limitless or endlessness, where there is something that is, at least, endless.

Beyond this there is No-thing; and beyond that, the Absolute. These three stages constitute a condensing, a crystallising out of the Being who permeates the whole of All, from a point in the centre of a circumferenceless sphere. This distillation, this point, is without dimension either in time or space, yet it contains all the Worlds, from the uppermost realm down through the Ladder of Creation to the lower end which is composed of space, gas, galactic clusters, galaxies, stars, planets, organic life, man, organs, cells, molecules, atoms and the sub-atomic realms down to that zone where matter ceases to be solid and becomes first energy, then an illusive nothing again.

This all-inclusive dot is called the First Crown, the first indication of the Absolute, perhaps better known as I AM, the first of many God names.

Out of this top Crown stream all the beings who have ever been, are or will be. Contained in the negative existence beyond lie myriads of possibilities. Man sees only a thin section of this ever-present dimension. In him are all his children and his children's children. Out of Adam came all men. Did Abraham guess at the full meaning of his seed becoming a nation? No one except perhaps the wisest can perceive what lies within him, what is present at that point in a negative form, ready to manifest tomorrow or a million years from now.

This is negative existence, that which is there but not there, that which by its very nature is the closest yet is the hardest to see. Here the Absolute is separate from his creation yet is ever-present within it.

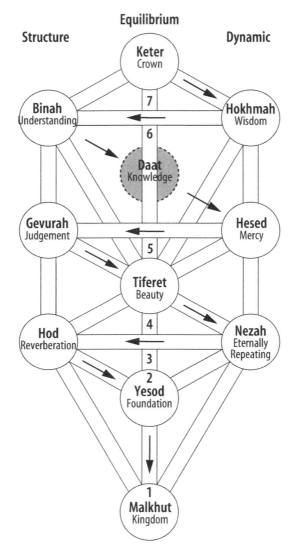

*Figure 11—LIGHTNING FLASH*
*In this diagram the Tree of Life, as it is called, is emanated by a downward flow that produces the Divine Numbers, or sefirot, and the twenty-two paths that connect them. The Hebrew names are but Biblical terms that give just a hint about their complex functions. Out of this operation emerge the triads that will be detailed in later Trees. This archetypal configuration is the basis of Kabbalah, in that every entity in Existence is called forth, created, formed and made according to its laws. There are seven levels within the Tree, anchored on the central column. (Halevi).*

# 3. *Lightning Flash*

The structure of the Tree of Life is based on the emanations flowing down from the first Crown. After the initial impetus of Creation a sequence unfolds from the first sefirah (or container) through eight stages to resolve in the tenth sefirah known as Malkhut, or the Kingdom, at the bottom of the central pillar.

This prime development might be likened to a musical octave from Do to Do with each note fulfilling a particular function as the emanations interact between energy and form, as expressed by the right and left pillars of the Tree of Life.

This progression is known as the Lightning Flash as it zig-zags down the tree. Beginning with Keter, the Crown, it flows towards Hokhmah (Wisdom) where it manifests itself as a potent dynamic at the top of the active column headed by Abba, the cosmic father or male principle. It then crosses to Binah (Understanding) which, as Aima the cosmic mother, heads the female column. The active and passive columns are also called the pillars of Severity and Mercy, the latter being the male. Here the Trinity of Creation begins to function as the divine energy out of perfect equilibrium seeks to find its level and resolve again. The flow of emanations, not diminished in essential nature though transforming into another order, then crosses the central column of equipoise and passes on to the sefirah Hesed (Mercy). Here the power, on being received into the active column again, takes on the dynamic expansive quality of this stage before emanating across to Gevurah (Judgement) in the fifth station. Here the force is checked, balanced and adjusted before being passed on to Tiferet, the vital sefirah on the middle pillar of the Tree. At this juncture there is a critical point of equilibrium. Tiferet, or Beauty, has a special relationship with Keter the Crown by connection through the axis of the central column. The only thing that separates Tiferet from Keter is an unseen sefirah known as Daat, or Knowledge, which functions only in particular conditions. At Tiferet an image is held. It is a mirror of Keter but operating on a lower scale. The emanations are then passed into the active sefirah Nezah or Eternity. This is the point where active functions repeat and repeat to maintain the energy level. From this transformer the emanations cross to Hod (Splendour). This may be also translated from the Hebrew root word as Reverberation which is, perhaps, a better description of the function of Hod whose job is to pick up and pass on information. From here the emanations again touch the central column and focus on Yesod or the Foundation. Here they are again mirrored but more dimly, being a reflection of a reflection, yet powerful enough to cast a strong projection—but only a projection. Directly below is the last sefirah, Malkhut, the Kingdom. In this are accumulated all the energies, active and passive, and all the processes received from the sefirot above. This is the resolving Do of the completed octave.

The sefirot on the Tree might be regarded as a system of functions in a circuit through which flows a divine current. Each function creates not only phenomena but transforms all the adjacent sub-circuits. Any sefirah can change the direction of flow, creating variable fields and actions. Power may be stepped up or down in all sefirot thereby modifying events, while the current returns to Source via the Earth of Malkhut.

An example of the Lightning Flash passing down the Tree is seen in the process of writing a book. Keter is the Crown, the creative principle. The idea is conceived in Hokhmah. As a vision it can be very powerful, the seed of a great novel, but in Hokhmah it is merely an idea, potent but formless. Over a long period it will begin to formulate in Binah. Perhaps it is better as a play or a film? Maybe as a story, short and to the point? Time and the principle of the top receptive sefirah of Binah shapes it into a book of, say, medium length, centred on a particular situation in which certain characters will participate. At this stage it may be held for years in a writer's mind, perhaps never to be written. But one day it may focus into a definite entity with a grand design. This is Daat, knowledge. From that time on there begins a quite new process which is called 'cooking' by some writers. The incubation period is followed by the Hesedic or gestating action and has the quality of great growth and expansion. Situations crop up, fragments of conversation intrude into the writer's consciousness, characters begin to develop of their own accord, the whole story begins to fill out and overflow. It is at this Hesed point of the operation that the writer must get to work or lose, by sheer mental dissipation, ideas welling up inside him. He begins to write an outline, setting down the creative forces present in him. However, he must continually judge and assess (the function of Gevurah) what the Hesed gives him, for it is often more than he needs and so a constant editing comes into the action. Gradually the book begins to take form and the essence, or Tiferet, starts to show. Maybe it is the great work of the century, the distillation of a lifetime's experience, perhaps it is just a humble textbook on stage property making, but it still has its stamp, its quite distinct quality. This is how we distinguish a Tolstoy from a Hemingway. In Tiferet the synthesis of form and energy is centred on the middle column and here is the reason why this sefirah is known as Beauty. However, at this point the book is still hardly visible. It is mainly in existence in the mind of the writer. He has to set it down in its entirety or it is just another unwritten masterpiece. Nezah, or Eternity, does this task. The vital forces of the body, controlled by Hod, the voluntary processes, make the pen move over the paper. Nezah knows its job instinctively while Hod, trained in mental and physical reflexes, focuses the acquired knowledge or language into what will be intelligible sentences. Yesod or the Foundation, which is an amalgam of all that has gone before, organises the whole operation in a personal style and reflects back what has been written while retaining a memory image for reference. Malkhut is the body and the book itself, the actual physical manifestation in the world. Heaven has reached Earth.

Here in this illustration we have a brief outline of the Lightning Flash as described in the Human Tree of Life. All creative processes in the Universe follow the same pattern, though in the terms of their own level.

# 4. *Tree and Man*

The Tree is said to underlie any complete being or organisation. How does it then relate to man? For it is most important that one verifies knowledge directly with one's experience or it becomes merely information.

Beginning at Keter as the unknown full potential of man, we follow the Lightning Flash in its zig-zag path down through the being of man.

In Hokhmah (Wisdom), we find the function of the inner intellect. This is the deepest part of the mind, the highest intellectual centre from which emanates silent thought. From this potent area the most profound ideas and observations come. This centre sees with the inner eye of illumination and speaks without words as Wisdom. It has an almost divine quality and indeed it has direct connection with the Divine World. Originality is its hallmark and in most people is only experienced a few times in a lifetime. It is said that epilepsy, the divine disease, is the state produced when a man suddenly has an excess of Hokhmah and blacks out as the rest of his organism cuts off the blast of light. In the rare case it may manifest as a flash of genius or the closing steps of Enlightenment.

Counterbalancing on the passive column is Binah, outer intellect or Understanding. As the name implies this sefirah stands under and receives. It is feminine and responds as a formulation to the active input coming across the Tree from Hokhmah and down the path from Keter. It resolves by receptive intelligence the communications into understandable principles. This is a lengthy procedure, sometimes taking many years. Einstein said that he saw certain ideas in a moment but had to spend a long period working them out, to get back to the original conception. This time factor is a quality of Binah. Besides receiving from above, Binah also responds to the flow coming from below. Experience in the outer world accumulates in Binah as understanding and an event observed many times is seen in terms of an overall view. 'It always happens that way', says the outer intellect. Constructively taken this is useful for seeing the grand design but thoughtlessly used it constitutes a too generalised and conservative outlook. Here we see how emphasis on one side of the Tree or the other results in a reactionary approach on the passive column or a revolutionary one on the active side. Neither are balanced but must be centred on the middle pillar of equilibrium. Binah, in this case, acts as the counterpoise to Hokhmah and *vice versa*. This occurs all the way down the Tree, each side checking the other. Binah is reflective thinking, to back up inspiration. It is method, the setting out of principle, the long view and the appreciation of cosmic processes and patterns. We see these two upper sefirot working in wise old men and sometimes in the deeper parts of ourselves. In cosmic terms they are our father and mother, both in physical and psychological as well as spiritual terms.

Hesed is inner emotion, the quality of devotion observed in a lifetime's work, the depth experienced perhaps in one love affair or the sense of feeling touched on in a profound religious moment. This sefirah in man represents a powerful creative urge, the kind of force that will make a people develop an idea, devote time and money to good works, give loving care to a demanding family or spend conscientious attention on the practice of an art. It is the emotional mainspring, the deep-water current that a man draws on for resource when ordinary emotions are inadequate. This is the place where magnanimity originates and from where higher emotion rises up.

Hesed in man is another inner voice. It is not the valued judgement of Gevurah, its outer emotional complement on the Tree. Hesed has the quality of mercy and generosity. However, overbalanced it can become a deluge of feeling, a drowning love, a benign despot who sees his licence as a right, tolerating anything. In this unbalanced state a man dissipates his wealth and health in indulgence, his lack of Gevurah or judgement allowing complete *laissez-faire*. A little less extreme is the Hesed-centred intellectual who will take up an overly liberal position. He will quote, usually from a secure Hesedic material situation, ideals about universal freedom and the brotherhood of man while his less fortunate fellows are oppressed by criminals taking advantage of his lack of vigilance.

Gevurah—outer emotion—is the counterweight in the emotional pair of opposites. Its function, sometimes defined traditionally as Severity, is to judge from moment to moment as one does in everyday matters. Ideally Gevurah should be impartial but no man has this factor built in. It has to be developed by the balance and interaction between the positive and negative sides of the Tree. This desire for equilibrium

38

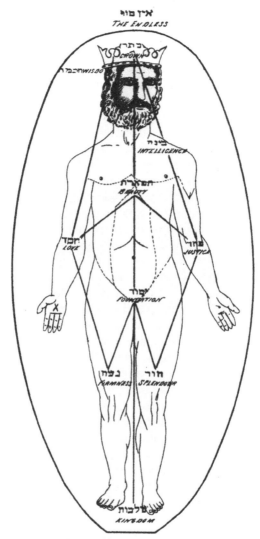

*Figure 12—ADAM KADMON*
*The primordial Tree of Life is also depicted symbolically as a humanoid figure. This is based upon Ezekiel's vision of a fiery Man seated upon the Throne of Heaven. This Divine Adam is said to be the image of God, the first reflection or manifestation of God beholding God. As can be seen in this picture, the ten sefirot are related to this radiant body. At this point it is but a sketch outline of a SELF portrait yet to be filled in by the experience and evolution of humanity which makes up the cells of this emanating archetype, Adam Kadmon, who precedes the Spiritual Adam created in Genesis. (From Ginsberg's Kabbalah, 19th century).*

is sought throughout Creation in all Worlds. It is also expressed in the traditional name of the middle pillar of 'Clemency' which stands between the columns of Severity and Mercy.

With Gevurah should come passive assessment. It receives the emanations from Binah above and, together with its own experience, forms a judgement which, according to the philosophy worked out or accepted by Binah, may range from the orthodox to the eccentric. Even an anarchist has his Binah and makes this his point of reference for his judgement. One only has to observe a heated political discussion to see Binah and Gevurah at work.

In its relation to Hesed, Gevurah works correctly as the feminine aspect. Like Binah, Gevurah responds also to the external world. Listen when meeting somebody new and you will hear your Gevurah present an unvoiced critique on everything about them. Behind this is, perhaps, your forgiving Hesed while above an often conventional Binah sets the background for the opinions. Of course these are very mundane reactions but for most of us they are the only ones we can easily identify as different parts of our psyche.

Gevurah unchecked, that is without the balancing element of magnanimity from Hesed, becomes positively aggressive instead of receptively sharp. Uncontrolled it can turn a man into a bigot, a disciplinarian or a cruel partisan. This is the sefirah of Aye or Nay, as a servant excellent, as a master militant and dangerous. In terms of larger human affairs it is the institutions which decide, under law — Binah — what is right and wrong. In social reforms it is the forces that clear away hypocrisy and corruption. On the individual level Gevurah destroys lies and disease, a vital function in any mind or organism. Overactive Gevurah talks in the Inquisition and McCarthyism while the passive Hesed advocates licence in whatever field is being discussed whether it is economics, ethics, social custom or the arts. Here once more emerges the necessary principle of reconciliation embodied in the middle pillar, sometimes also known as the column of mildness.

Tiferet (Beauty) is the focus of the essential nature of a man. It lies on the central column, the axis of consciousness which flows up and down from Keter to Malkhut. In man, the height at which he is centred on this column determines the level of his being and, while the two columns on either side perform functions, the column of equilibrium shows what he is.

One's essential nature is that with which a man is born. It is his very own yet it partakes of the realms above and the kingdoms below. Tiferet has been described as Keter on a lower level or, in Biblical terms, a man in God's image. Tiferet is that which is most real in an individual. Here at the focus of eight paths is the synthesis embodied in Tiferet. Known traditionally as the Seat of Solomon, it has access to all the sefirot except Malkhut (Kingdom) or in man, his body. That is why a man's essential nature cannot be seen in the physical world, though its character may be traced in his actions.

Tiferet, Beauty or the essential nature of a man, is his consciousness of himself. He knows of himself, though he may forget it most of the time, so involved is he in activity. It is the watcher in moments of great danger. It is the observer who sees without eyes, whose awareness marks moments with a strange lucidity. Here is what you are, a reflection of I AM.

Tiferet is called Beauty and not without reason. It is the point of equilibrium, the perfect symmetrical centre of the Tree of Life. If you wish to examine any complete organism, place it on the slide plate of Tiferet and the Tree will act as a microscope. Using this essential crystal all the aspects will find their places on the Tree, each sefirah demonstrating, through its principle and function, the structure and organisation of the thing you are examining.

In man his essential nature is his key. 'Know thyself' say all philosophers. In Tiferet is this self, poised halfway between Heaven and Earth. Embedded in the body for a time it partakes of the upper and lower Worlds, bringing the Divine down into Matter and raising matter up towards Spirit. Tiferet is at the juncture of the visible and the invisible. When you meet a man you have not seen for twenty years, his physical appearance may have changed profoundly since you saw him at school, yet you recognise him without question. Is it the features? The eyes? No—it is something else, quite personal to him and even after eighty years still peculiarly his own. This is the essential nature shining out of the man.

This sefirah has a special place. It is a point into which things flow from all directions and flow out again. Without Tiferet or a man's essential nature the body of Malkhut would be a soulless automaton, a mere system of divine plumbing with no possibility of evolution. Tiferet, then, is the nodal point of growth. Every lesson learned is fed into this sefirah, slowly raising its level from a dormant being into an active fully grown, awakened participator within the person. This is perhaps the meaning of the story of the Sleeping Beauty and all her slumbering court. As a Tree of Life we are the palace, the princess and all the courtiers. But where is the prince?

Above Tiferet on the axis of consciousness lies the invisible sefirah of Daat or Knowledge. Placed below the Crown, it represents in man the point where he does not just know of, but is. It is in this instant that his individuality vanishes and he may experience—or non-experience—union with the Divine Keter. At rare moments in meditation, we are told, such a phenomenon occurs. One vanishes not into dreams, as is mostly the case, but into nothing—or No-thing. A man who attains this state might well describe a void, an abyss in which the ego dies. From this we get many misunderstood commentaries about the annihilation of the Self. Perhaps the nearest parallel in ordinary life is of love when the lover totally forgets himself in the beloved, only in this case the 'dark mistress' Shakespeare speaks of in the sonnets does not sue for breach of promise once the affair is over. This love is of a cosmic order, the first step in the courtship between the heavenly bridegroom of Keter and his bride in earthly Malkhut. Daat is the veil, beyond which lies knowledge and being of the Objective Universe.

Nezah—Eternity or the 'repeating' sefirah—is, in man, all the involuntary physical and psychological processes. It is the first sefirah actually to be seen at work in the physical realm. Nezah, at the root of the active column of the Tree, provides the force for all the vital functions, ranging from the heartbeat to the digestive processes of the gut. This sefirah not only manifests in all the inward cyclic processes but in the outward too—the instinct of attraction and repulsion between the sexes, the ebb and flow of desires. Here is Nature at work, creative, forever building up then dissolving, circling a myriad tiny daily changes that are linked with the motions of the external year. In Nezah resides love but of a different order from that of Hesed above. This instinctive love emerges each Spring when thousands upon thousands of young men suddenly become attached to young women, each one of course a unique relationship to those concerned. This phenomenon has been observed over many centuries with delight, the mature realising that it is part of a cycle, an eternally repeating Spring festival in the body of mankind.

Nezah in the human organism is the provider of the instinctive powerhouse. It maintains not only the body's health but provides energy for Hod, the voluntary processes, the counterbalance on the receptive side of the Tree. Hod, as we have said, may be translated

42

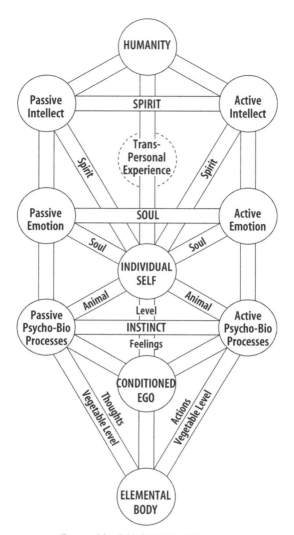

*Figure 13—PSYCHE IN GENERAL*
*Here the human mind is placed upon the Tree. Beginning at the bottom are the physical levels of the four states of matter. Above this is the vegetable part of the mental organism, as it is strongly influenced by the body. Over this comes the animal component of the psyche with all its impulses and primitive intelligence. Beyond the domain of the ego is the Self at the heart of, in most cases, the unconscious of a person. This comprises the emotions and the intellect which are not to be confused with ordinary ego-centric feelings and thoughts. Here are the central inner triads of the soul, spirit and Divine. At the Crown is the connection with the collective origin of humanity.* (Halevi).

from the Hebrew as 'Splendour', but its root also lies in the word 'Reverberation'. The root word of Hod applies very precisely to the voluntary processes. This includes all the senses which can be directed outwards and respond or reverberate to incoming data. Beside the obvious five receptors, man is not only sensitive to heat, smell, sound and all other physical impressions, he is also open to the meaning contained within the sound of words, music, the marks seen as mathematics, symbols and forms. A man may receive physical, emotional and intellectual stimuli, all of which need to be communicated to the interior world of the organism. Thus a remarkable abstract concept or the sight of a naked girl may have great impact on a man and yet not be received by the same sefirot within him. The excitement generated in these two cases could be Hod and Nezah respectively, though not necessarily in other situations.

Besides responding to the outer world, as does the whole of the passive column of which Hod is the bottom rung, this sefirah also checks Nezah. A man may find a certain girl unbearably attractive but Hod controls his desire. This is the sefirah of mental input or education as well. Good conventional manners are assimilated here as are all acquired skills which are then stored in the brain to become conditioned memories and reflexes, be they general knowledge or physical responses. A soldier's training in arms may be second nature in battle but it still belongs to Hod, though his desire to survive is Nezah.

These two lowest sefirot provide the manifestation of the active and passive principles in the physical realm which begins at this point on the Tree. The Nezah-Hod level and below is what we normally see of the world. Observe a rush hour scene in a big city. Everyone's eyes are blank, far away in dreams, as their Hod-Nezah systems guide them without fail along routine paths. In work and leisure Hod and Nezah carry out endless tasks, operating machines, reading, writing, running a home, bringing up children, socialising, playing physical or intellectual games and making love. Between and below these two lowest of the functional sefirot lies the Universe of our mundane perception. Yesod is the mind pivot of the world of materiality and action, ego consciousness on the middle pillar. Its English name, 'Foundation', indicates its importance in perceiving the Universe about us.

Yesod, in man, relates to that strange part of him wherein he forms images. On the central column but on a lower scale than Tiferet, it is like a screen-mirror continually reflecting and projecting into the ordinary consciousness what is presented by the paths flowing into it.

*Figure 14—LEVELS*
*Every human being has four levels within themselves. A person can choose which one will dominate their life. The bottom-most is the mineral state in which a person can remain inert and just be like a stone, only moved by external circumstances. The next level is that of the vegetable. Here the man or woman only seeks security, comfort and a mate to propagate the species. Animal people are compulsive competitors who desire to beat all others by being the most powerful, rich or beautiful. The truly and fully human beings are those who develop their souls and spirits so as to serve a higher purpose than themselves.* (Medieval woodcut).

These paths hold it in position amid the four points of Tiferet, Nezah, Hod and Malkhut and through it a man sees the inner and outer Worlds. Yesod is supplied by data coming from Hod, energy from Nezah and the physical vehicle in which to live by Malkhut. Ideally it is the servant of Tiferet, the essential nature which is, in turn, but the steward of a man for whom Keter (Crown) is King. However, as so often happens, a man forgets quite early in childhood the lucid observer of his essential nature and begins only to trust Yesod, the ever-accumulating ego persona which his world and those about him wish him to acquire. If he comes from one stratum of society it will take on this form, if from another, that. Moreover, his family will require that he behaves this way, his school friends that. These and other habits and attitudes are assimilated in his Yesod and form his picture of himself, an artefact ego. While Hod supplies the material in his response to the external world and Nezah to the inner, his imitation and comparisons of what he perceives will build up a picture of his relationship to life about him. His attractions and repulsions create yet another form which is lodged in the psychological Yesodic armour slowly accreting over his essential nature, partly to protect it and partly to imprison. This is the *persona*, Latin for mask, a quite accurate description for what is called personality. Here is what the world sees and sometimes, with a man who has lost touch with himself, what he himself thinks is his true nature. A face may be bland and the manner charming but to the discerning eye this may be a man imprisoned in a psychological iron mask.

Yesod is, in its correct position, a superb minister. It gathers in all the information from the physical and psychological realms and focuses it into readable images. Thus you remember scenes with sounds and smells, recall telephone numbers, set out the elements of a problem to be solved, replay or rehearse a situation that has been or is to be enacted. It is a reflector of what cannot be seen directly of the psyche or body. It is a personal mental read-out screen for a working scientist and the inner projection room for an artist. Yesod presents a fragile ephemeral structure held in equilibrium on the lowest rung of consciousness. In sleep it runs a midnight newsreel movie of the day and the current problems, often using actors and settings supplied by other sefirot. In the case of madness, Yesod appears to be the real world because the connection with Malkhut below is blocked or severed. On death Yesod is said to rewind the film of a man's life before him. Though not proven it is an interesting speculation.

46

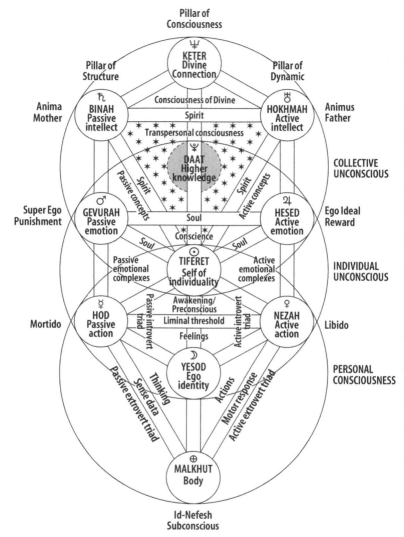

*Figure 15—PSYCHE IN DETAIL*
*Here the triads are filled out to reveal the active and passive aspects of the mind.*
*These contain personal memories and cultural concepts, such as childhood experience*
*or the class into which one was born. Social conditioning creates what is called the*
*super ego, or that which is forbidden by the clan, in contrast to the ego ideal which*
*propagates what is expected and is admired. The three circles define how various*
*levels of the mind interrelate while the triads of the soul and spirit reveal the inner*
*dimensions of the mind, leading to the consciousness of the Divine. At the very bottom*
*is the Id-Nefesh or vital soul of the body. (Halevi).*

Yesod, then, is a fixed mask outwards and a chameleon mirror inwards, the mask's configuration distorting or clarifying the picture presented to the inner consciousness. Here is held a man's body image, the awareness of just how long his arms are, the knowledge of how much he can raise his voice to get a desired effect. This is a linking reference arena for all he has learnt, so that if he is a savage or a sophisticate he can at least recognise the physical or intellectual clothes he wears. However, like the Emperor's new suit, it is not always as substantial as he would like to believe for though it appears solid, it is but a useful mirage borrowed for a lifetime to deal with familiar contexts but when confronted with an important decision out of its field of reference it is quite inadequate. Observe yourself when two friends from totally different spheres meet you off your home ground. A mild schizophrenia occurs—this is the persona or one or two aspects of it—whereas a man in touch with his essential nature is the same to everyone. Yesod can be a bridge or a barrier. It can be the vehicle of creative imagination or a retreat for illusion. It is the principal view we have of ourselves and the world. Dependent on the dullness or translucence of the screen-mirror, the active or passive state of our mask, we are on the bottom rung of consciousness. The choice is to wake up or remain half asleep.

The second and just as important feature of Yesod, the Foundation, in its relation to man, is its correspondence to the sexual act. This sefirah, situated on the main axis of the Tree, receives power directly via Tiferet from Daat and Keter. Focused in Yesod, with the inflowing from the male and female sides of the Tree, it makes the sexual triad. This is because the active-passive forces are brought into creative relationship by the pillar of equilibrium. True, the three pairs of outer sefirot are higher on the Tree but they are primarily functional opposites. Only the central sefirot can take on the unique rôle of transformation.

Yesod can trigger conception in sexual union and it is also the conscious basis or foundation of spiritual birth. Tiferet is concerned with the discovery of the Self while Daat is the point where that identity vanishes in the void of cosmic consciousness before union with Keter.

In outer life Yesod is the great driving force. Sex is more than just the act, it generates more than children. Commerce and the arts know that men love women and women adore men. Advertising, films, plays, restaurants, clothes, a myriad activities are devoted to this mutual dynamic that gives the drama of life its spice. The machine age will never replace the interaction between the sexes and the vast amount of time and energy spent on it. The driving force of Yesod is found in politics as well as the dance hall. Men strive to prove themselves by getting to the top of the heap and even the highly technical operation of reaching the Moon has a strong dream and phallic-Yesodic-quality.

This powerhouse is vital to life. Without it a man has no strength to draw upon. Energy may flow down from above but here is a choice of direction. Through the conversion of this abundant force a man may take a step up the ladder of Self-realisation, begin his return. He will, if he does, move in opposition to the descending octave of Creation and retrace the path back to Creation's source. Perhaps this is why this sefirah is called Foundation.

Malkhut, in man, is his physical body. The English translation, Kingdom, refers to the terrestrial elements. The body is composed literally of earth, all the bones, tissues and cells constructed of mineral and traces of metal with enough iron for a fair-sized nail, we were told at school. These Earth elements form, for the most part, the structure of the body and are held in position like a standing wave, in as much as they sustain the body's form and systems while continually changing its substance.

The principle embodied in the Water element also continually passes through the organic standing wave known as the body. In blood and all the body fluids water circulates every zone, passing not only along the finest-gauge capillaries but through cell walls. Without the element Water the body would shrivel up, cease the vital exchanges found in metabolism. These internal tides not only maintain the easy flow of the material passing into and out of the body but help in the process of growth.

Air, the third elemental state, is manifest as a major contributor to the energy-generating cycle of the body but it is also to be seen as the various gases present. These may permeate blood and tissue and deprivation of one gaseous element may cause a serious imbalance, even death. Man, prior to birth, is an aquatic creature, living in the fluids of the womb. At birth, with the first breath comes a distinct quantum jump into mammal life, even if no other development follows. In the air, besides the well-known gases, are several others, some very rare and difficult to trace. It is said that in an awakened spiritual state the body can extract these fine elements, precipitating yet another birth—but this time of consciousness.

Fire, the lightest element, is a symbol for radiance, flame emitting heat, light and many other frequencies. In man this might be seen as that property which permeates the whole organism and which is so obviously absent in a corpse. It might, in one state, be heat or, in another, the bio-electrical envelope which surrounds the living. It could be seen as psychological illumination. It is, however, discernible as the subtlest materiality present in the physical body. The electrical fields within living cells might only be the crudest description of a vibratory process emanating from the DNA molecules composing and governing them. These molecules in turn may only be the printed circuits for receiving that curious influx of energy known as Life, for it is apparent that when any organism is cut off from Nature or the vital radiance of the Sun it droops from lack of stimulating input and with complete deprivation of whatever Fire on Earth is, it dies.

For man, Malkhut is also the physical Universe. When he looks out through a telescope or down a microscope he sees Malkhut, the densest level of Materiality. Even his radio telescopes only register Malkhut — the physical radiant fields surrounding celestial bodies. The fine pictures of the galaxy Andromeda are but the photographs of a quite solid body in a defused state. And electron microscope pictures of atomic structures merely film their physical appearance, though we might guess at why they form those latticed patterns. The next realm, that of the Universe of Formation, lies out of physical sight closer to the vision seen in an artist's studio than in a scientific laboratory.

Malkhut is the world with which we are most familiar, for men tend to see results rather than causes. Preferring the end product, as it is now fixed, we often forget the actions that created it. The Rembrandts scattered about the art galleries of the world are the residue of his creative process, the dim physical sketch of what he really saw. In Malkhut, however, is all that went before; it contains every quality of all the sefirot concentrated into matter. The whole of natural evolution is present in a man's body. Every organic stage from conception has to be passed through before human birth. With maturity, when Nature has completed her job of outfitting, the next evolutionary process of consciousness is taken on by a man himself.

The Kabbalists have a saying: 'In Keter is Malkhut and Malkhut is in Keter'. This can be taken many ways but in this case it is like the analogue of a seed. Within the tough dense kernel of a chestnut resides not just one possible new tree but a whole forest of generations.

Another meaning is that within the thickest of matters is spirit; imprisoned, yes, but present and always ready for the re-ascent back to the Absolute. This is Malkhut, the lowest of the sefirot yet the most loaded with potential. In man, within the vehicle of his physical body, is the possibility of rapid development. In the difficult situation of life on Earth, maximum resistance creates great potential and therefore possibilities. This is backed by all the resources locked up within man. A delicate but tough mechanism, the body, soul and spirit is a fantastic powerhouse full of many different kinds of fuel, each with a particular function and quality. The millions of parts and sophisticated systems of the first rocket to the Moon were crude compared to just the machine part of a man and he is designed to go higher, even beyond the Sun.

Looking back at the Tree of Life in terms of man, we see it as a living organism, each sefirah balancing its complement and contributing to a whole integrated system. By study of ourselves we may recognise the various parts and even observe occasionally from which sefirah we began a thought, a feeling or an action. This will be studied later in detail as we become more familiar with the diagram.

One final word. The Tree, when superimposed on a man, reveals that we only see a fraction of his nature. Besides his body and personality, the rest of him is invisible to the physical world. With the aid of the Tree of Life we may come to perceive his soul. Time allows us a glimpse of him but the baby, the child, and adolescent he was are gone and what he might be has not yet come. The Tree is the only permanent feature in a man, in that he is modelled on an eternal universal design. This is the full man, containing all Creation, and in the image of God who made him.

# 5. *Tree and Gods*

Having related the sefirot to man, we now apply the ancient maxim 'As above so below' to demonstrate the Tree of Life on another dimension. Taking the Sky as a larger World and using the argument that what was loosely called the macrocosm is modelled on the same universal plan, Kabbalists described the Tree in terms of the Greco-Roman gods and their corresponding planets. This enabled the Tree to be viewed in wider vision using the myths about the gods to describe the sefirot. In addition to this, the Solar system was arranged as an organism but seen from the position of Earth which is centred appropriately in Malkhut, the lowest sefirah. This fitted into the Ptolemaic world picture which, contrary to modern scientific belief, was not a naïve picture of the Solar system but a relative framework (the only basic one we have in a vast universe) as seen from man's situation. This geocentric scheme, combined with the Tree, was one of the earliest theories of relativity, taking into account not only the physical positions of the heavenly bodies but also their functional relationship within the Solar system.

Beginning this time with Malkhut, we start with Mother Earth or, in kabbalistic terms, the Bride. Situated at the bottom of the Tree it is the realm of the elements. In concrete physics, it is a rocky ball of minerals and metals covered with a skin of water, surrounded by an atmosphere of air and the electro-magnetosphere radiating far out into space.

This layered coat of radiation is the Fire element of the Earth. Together these various states of matter, solid, liquid, gas and radiation, form the body of the planet. Deep inside it, on or near the hard surface, is a thin living film called Nature which contains not only the flora and fauna of Pan but this strange creature called man, the most sensitive organism of natural evolution.

Malkhut is our physical environment. Embedded in it we lose sight of it. As our bodies are composed of it, we forget it is a temporary form through which the four elemental states pass. At death the physical mould is broken and the elements disperse, each to its own level in the

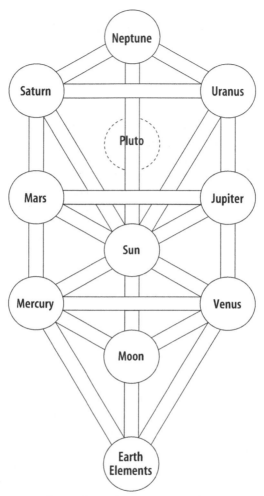

*Figure 16—GODS AND PLANETS*
*The gods and planets were well known to the Jews of the ancient world. Indeed, Abraham came from the city of Ur of the Chaldees, the city of astrologers. Here the Solar system is set out on the Tree according to medieval Kabbalah. Later, the outer planets were added to the upper sefirot. The reason is that the astrological character of celestial bodies seems to match the sefirot. Clearly the Sun and Moon relate to the Self and the ego while the inferior planets of Mercury and Venus can be equated with the psycho-physical part of the mind. Mars and Jupiter, likewise, correspond to the emotional poles with Saturn and Uranus concurring with the active and passive qualities of the intellect. Neptune and Pluto do fit well on the central column as degrees of higher consciousness. They rule Pisces and Scorpio, two of the most mystic signs. (Halevi).*

planet. Malkhut is the Bride, the great Terrestrial Mother recognised by all civilisations, be they agricultural or industrial. Gaea, the Greek Earth Mother, was the great provider and nourisher. Without her men, animals and plants could not live and she had to be wooed and husbanded for raw material and food. Female by nature, this sefirah adapts and adopts the character of the influences converging upon it. However, passive and immobile as it might appear this maternal, elemental kingdom is the womb of spirit being reborn. Malkhut is what science might call physics and though crude in relation to metaphysics it is the elemental end of a vast cosmic spectrum. In Greek mythology, out of Gaea the Great Earth Mother was born Uranus, the starry sky and out of their union came the Giant Titans, one of whom was Chronos, known to us in Latin as Saturn—the God of Time.

About the Earth its satellite Luna, the Moon, orbits. Enclosed within the planet's gravitational and magnetic field the Moon's pull, in counter balance, not only drags the Earth's seas up and down but draws all the fluids within every living thing, so that Nature responds in a daily and monthly rhythm of ebb and flow. Plants grow in monthly pulses as they expand and contract their spreads, the moisture content of their sap waxing and waning in their tissue.

Animals on land and in the sea are affected by these lunar fluctuations, their hunting and breeding habits coinciding with the Moon's phases.

Men, too, are influenced, the cycles of crime in big city police records showing a monthly rise and fall. Blood coagulates faster at certain Lunar times and anyone who has worked in an asylum will know the distinct restlessness that occurs at full Moon.

Fable has it that Selene, goddess of the Moon, though ruler of the realm of Pan, loved Endymion the shepherd who represented mankind. However, she could only love him through his sleep, reach him through his dreams—or the sefirah of Yesod. Here also lies the pendulum of Nature's mechanism, in humanity the regulation of mass cycles and in the individual, personal moods.

In Diana the huntress and Artemis the multi-breasted goddess the Moon's birth-death aspects are shown, each deity describing respectively the new and full nodal points in the Lunar appearance. This constantly altering shape and size is created by the Moon's motion along the Zodiac as she progresses through her daily rising and setting. Besides these motions, she wanders back and forth across the celestial equator and occasionally looms nearer to Earth, thus completing the impression of an endless variation within a system of revolutions. From a kabbalistic viewpoint we see the principle of eternal change, the Moon's position in relation to the Earth and Sun continually altering the mask of reflection. In man's psyche we see the same thing—the Yesodic screen-image is never the same yet it repeats endlessly in variation. Under certain conditions the Moon is evocative of romance and all the fascination that love-song and story tell but daylight and down-to-earth facts break the illusion when the reality of a child's conception, and its subsequent complications, dawn. The lunatic, aptly named, lives exclusively within this realm of imagination, the sefirah of Yesod. In his case he is disconnected from Malkhut, the world outside.

Yesod, here represented by the Moon, is also sex and governs, it is said, the female menstrual cycle. Another aspect—witchcraft, the applied use of the Yesodic energy and image-making—is symbolised in Hecate, the Lunar goddess of enchantments.

There are many facets to Yesod on this scale. For the Earth on this dimension Time is different. If we take one year or a complete round of the seasons as one breath measure for our planet, the Moon's orbit would appear as a whirling object circling the Earth.

Compared with the rest of the Solar system, the Earth and her large Moon are twins—in effect a single organisation or one being. To the other planets, the Earth might appear to wear a Lunar face (rather like a thicker version of Saturn's rings would seem to us), though to the Earth itself it would be but a see-through veil. Indeed a celestial twin, the Moon, nearest body to the Earth, is so close it acts like a reflective screen between us and outer space. Through this shimmering whirling mask every influence going out or coming in must pass. It is in the same position as the persona is to a man, lying correspondingly between the Sun of his essential nature and the Earth of his body. Bridge and barrier, the Moon both joins and separates, its pale screen reflecting what the Earth cannot directly look upon. In kabbalistic terms Yesod—the Moon—lies on the axis of consciousness but it is also at the lower meeting point, on the Tree, of the inflow from the combined active and passive influence of the planets.

Mercury, in the sefirah Hod, is the Messenger to the gods. He stands in astronomical terms nearest to Apollo the Sun. Through his orbit the Solar rays must pass before reaching any of the other planets. His is the sphere of transmission, having no potent force of his own because of his minute size. Mercury was also considered to take on

*Figure 17—INFLUENCES*
*Astrology, which is as old as Jewish mysticism and prophecy, is based upon centuries of observation on the influences of the cosmos. While the Sun and Moon clearly govern the seasons and the tides, it was also observed that the planets had an effect on events and individuals. In this Wheel of Fortune, Mars at the top makes people determined and sometimes precipitates war while Mercury here at the bottom is very weak, causing trade and personal communication to falter. Meanwhile, the influence of the Sun and Venus rises while Jupiter, Saturn and the Moon falls. Kabbalah sees those fluctuations as important factors in the human psyche and history.* (Medieval woodcut).

and enhance the qualities of the other planets with which he came into conjunction. His talent lay, it was said, in his flexibility—his Mercurial nature—which enabled him to adapt, modify, use and throw away whatever came into his field. He was the god of thieves and merchants, the rapid sleight of hand and of exchange and trade. He was the deity concerned with the acquisition of knowledge and its dispensation. Witty, cunning, deft, fleet of foot, all his qualities are of the essence of Hod—Reverberation or Splendour. As in the voluntary processes in man with his many senses, Mercury represents the versatile intelligence that scans for data, picks it up, passes it on, then scans again. Consider the ability and mechanism of the human eye and ear. In themselves they are always in movement, reverberating and transmitting information. With the gods, Mercury performed the same function, keeping them informed and informing in a continuous round of errands while amusing himself with endless games and love affairs. Of these the three most important were Persephone, an aspect of Mother Earth (Malkhut), Hecate, Moon goddess of witchcraft and childbirth (Yesod) and Aphrodite, Venus, the goddess of Nature (Nezah). All these compose the bottom triad of the Tree of Life with Mercury acting as the outer sensor or intelligence.

Mercury, besides being the Divine Herald, was also the receptacle of ordinary and extraordinary knowledge. Because of his ability to fly anywhere at great speed he knew about everything. This included geography, history, science, all the matters relating to study—the realm of Hod. Moreover, because he carried the caduceus, the rod entwined with two snakes, the symbol of his office, he had access to the knowledge about—I repeat—'about' metaphysics. The caduceus is another version of the Tree of Life. The rod is the pillar of equilibrium and each snake describes the active and passive principles passing down from the winged head of the rod to its foot. However, this is a book to be read and studied as an introduction, as are all of the treatises on the Hermetic (Hermes or Mercurial) sciences. Here is the theoretical field, the point of input necessary before practice. Mercury had many skills, ranging from handicrafts to the manipulation of ideas—all acquired. He was also a great liar and deceiver and in man one knows how the senses can also mislead when, for instance, a mercurial problem like an optical illusion is presented. Perhaps for this reason Mercury and the sefirah of Hod is the god and province of magicians, scientists and charlatans.

Astronomically, Mercury is only rarely seen for its motion is swift and too close to the Sun. Yet without its presence just outside the Sun's corona, who knows what the inner balance of the Solar system might be? As in the mechanics of a watch a hair spring, though light and fine, nevertheless governs, by its critical position and function, the delicate regulation of the whole mechanism. In man's body is the same thing, one extra grain of this or that substance may mean the difference between madness or sanity and the sefirah Hod keeps this balance in conjunction with Nezah.

Nezah is Venus in this view of the Tree of Life. Venus is the goddess of beauty, love and instinct. She is depicted as a naked woman, lovely in form. In her is embodied the power to stir desire. She is the goddess of Nature, spring and growth. Her power to arouse is partly centred in her grace—her preoccupation is with beauty, perhaps because of her marriage to the ugliest god on Olympus, Vulcan. The stories of her amorous affairs are endless, one continuous cycle of attraction and rejection. This could be a key to the kabbalistic designation 'Eternity'. Another could be the ever returning Spring which is her special domain. Here everything is renewed after the nadir of Winter. This is the vital impulse in the endless chain necessary to maintain Nature. Without courtship there would be no marriage, without the union no children to repeat the cycle of generation. Spring is the period of beauty, the Earth clothes herself with blossom and the creatures sing and dance in a great game of love. Man is subject to this vital impulse and many of his arts are devoted to the subject. Venus is the planet and goddess of the sefirah Nezah, her morning and evening star appearance marking the systole and diastole of a gentle cycle that is eternally pulsing through Nature and the Solar system. In man she represents the involuntary processes, such as the gut and heart. But Nezah also defines that which we find attractive and then repulsive. Venus's love adventures have this quality of seduction then rejection. There is never the stable consummation of a situation. Her being was concerned with ease, the effortless. Drudgery and strain were not in her experience. The heart pumps without thought and the stomach digests with no prompting and when either of these is troubled the organism is—as the very word explains—diseased.

Charm and grace are the attributes of Venus. From her the arts of music and painting come, as does poetry. Nezah is to the arts what Hod is to the sciences. However, while Hod observes, as the receptive side of the Tree, Nezah is on the active and this is why, though science is currently dominant, it cannot entirely reject the power of the arts

58

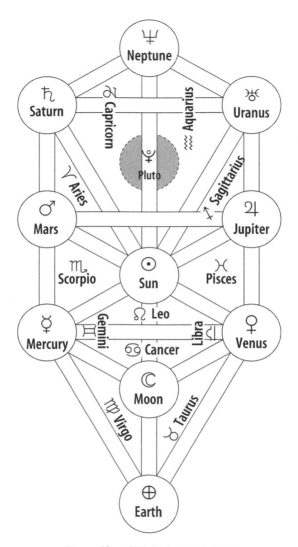

*Figure 18—ASTROLOGICAL TREE*
*Here the triads are related to signs of the zodiac. For example the Earth, Moon and*
*Mercury triangle is ruled by Virgo which is related to earthy, practical, analytical*
*thought; while the triad of Cancer, made up of Mercury, Venus and the Moon is*
*concerned with the ego's moods. The Leo triad on the central column of consciousness*
*relates, through the Sun, to Mars and Jupiter and the soul triad. The side triads and*
*signs define the psychological functions while Pluto and Neptune govern the central*
*spiritual and Divine triangles. These astrological symbols give much insight into how*
*the Tree and psyche work.* (Halevi).

which indicate the driving force in a community. The world's great books, pictures and music reveal more potently the mood of a given time than any machine or new discovery.

Venus is the counterbalance to Mercury and *vice versa*. It is the desire for a more pleasant standard of living that encourages science. Venus, or the power of love, it is said, makes the world go round. This cliché is more true than imagined. Without Nezah a man would not want to work, either for a new car, a fine house or a beautiful wife. This force is quite different from Yesodic energy. It is biological, natural, rooted in the need to give and receive, the reciprocal arrangement observed in the cell, man and Nature as a whole. Venus always seeks that which is desirable, away from the painful, whether it is hunger or what is uncomfortable; or towards the pleasant, be it a new love or a familiar pleasure in an eternal graceful roundabout.

The position of Tiferet in this cosmic scheme is occupied by the Sun. Tiferet in man is defined as the essential nature or the individual Self. This is Apollo in the central position of a man and the Solar system. Nearly all paths lead to Tiferet, feeding energy in, before they are radiated out again. In man this same sefirah could be called the Watcher in that it perceives directly into all the sefirot except Malkhut. Apollo was known as the god of Truth to the Greeks. Moreover, he was renowned for his outstanding awesome Beauty—which is the English translation for Tiferet. His Oracle at Delphi was famous for its penetrating answers, very apt for the God of Light.

Tiferet is the Sun, almost impossible to look upon directly. Such was the face of Apollo that a glance at it by the unprepared might blind them for life. Seen from the view of a man, this might well correspond to seeing more than a man could bear to know about himself. This is why most men live in Yesod—the Moon of themselves—preferring to see only by reflection the light of their real nature.

Astronomically the Sun lies at the centre of the Solar system. It is the pivot around which all the other planets turn. Modern scientists tell us that not only does it radiate heat, light and a large range of waves and particles but that it also absorbs, sucks in vast quantities of inter-stellar gas as it moves round the Milky Way. This could be seen as positive energy and negative matter coming in from the right and left columns of the Tree to feed the being embodied in the astronomical and psychological Sun.

The Sun not only illuminates all the planets but also shines light on the smallest particles the human eye can detect, so fine are its wave-lengths. Psychologically the same phenomenon occurs within a man who is in touch with his own being as focused in Tiferet. This *is* him. True, only a miniature being compared to Keter, as our Sun is to the Galaxy, but it is nevertheless his own individuality. This is Apollo, the god who could only speak the truth, whose silver bow could strike at any distance and yet whose golden lyre could delight the other gods. Apollo has an awesome aspect. In him is brilliance, the quality so often ascribed to great men. Enlightenment is a term not used idly or just for poetic reasons. It is a precise description of the nature of Tiferet, for it is the Sun of a man, the point exactly between Heaven and Earth, Keter and Malkhut, in him. Here spirit is half caught in form. It partakes of the upper and lower parts of the Tree, except where it is guarded from burning up the Earth by Yesod and from losing its temporary individuality by the invisible gate of Daat.

Apollo was considered as a direct link between the gods and men. His position on the Tree of Life and in the Solar system backs up this assertion. Through the Sun god, all the sefirot can be reached. In a man centred on his inner essential nature every part of his being may be known. Here is the Delphic Oracle in a person. Ask it a real question and it will reply—the simple Truth. This is the voice that speaks occasionally from our own inner depths of space. This is the interior Sun—the Apollo most of the time we dare not face for fear of his penetrating glance. Mercury, the myth says, stole from Apollo but by divination, that is, by direct perception, the thief was found out. Hod may be cunning, Nezah distracting with her pleasures, as Yesod is with her dreams, but ultimately Tiferet blasts through, if only at the moment before death.

Tiferet—Apollo—the Sun lies on the axis of consciousness. Through it passes the majority of forces flowing down the Tree and through the Solar system. Behind it lies the Sun of the Sun—Keter, the Crown—through which stream the Divine emanations.

Gevurah is symbolised in Mars, the traditional god and planet of war. These symbols, it would appear, were designed with great care by the ancient world, certainly with as much attention to detail as a modern computer or aero engine. If we examine each symbol and its component parts we will see they were not constructed by a vague superstitious collection of Greek witch-doctors but were the product of highly sophisticated thinking, each image a whole book in its own right. The chief difference between the ancient and modern way of looking at the Universe is scale and language. While we know much

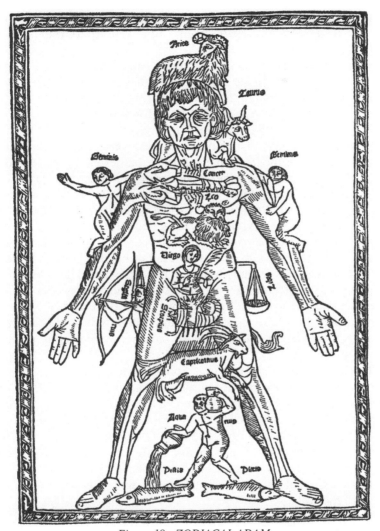

*Figure 19—ZODIACAL ADAM*

*By medieval times, astrology had become a very complex and sophisticated system, closely studied by Jews, Christians and Moslems. Here the archetypal image of a celestial human being corresponds at the cosmic level with the Divine Adam Kadmon. Indeed, the theory was that the microcosm of the individual on Earth, being made into the same image, resonated with what was going on in the Heavens. This could be seen in historic events and individual temperaments. For example, England always has difficult times when Saturn afflicts its Aries ascendant while people born under this sign are generally adventurers, ready to challenge or defend their ground, as well as be in the forefront of any enterprise.* (Medieval woodcut).

about size, great and small, they understood depth and dimension. This is seen very clearly in twenty-first century physics and its confusion.

In the symbol of Mars are many ideas. Superficially he seems only to mean strife but a closer look reveals that it always takes two to quarrel. Contention cannot happen on its own. This points to the dual aspect of the god, the Aye and Nay, the for and against, the pro and con. This is the essential quality of Gevurah. At this point on the Tree decisions are continually being made, comparisons set up and selections carried out. In its most dramatic form a battlefield is the deciding ground, one side or the other conquering. In man, his day-to-day emotional faculty is continually assessing, be it like or dislike of people, ideas or things. Its hallmark is a clear-cut judgement. This is Gevurah or the sword of Mars, dividing this from that with one quick cut while his shield parries and balances. This is the passive aspect of his nature.

Mars is sometimes known as ruthless but he also has been known to run from the field of battle howling, like a coward. This was usually when he was confronted by Pallas Athene, the war goddess whose coolness, courage and intelligence always got the better of Mars for, when roused, he tended to fly into a rage which reduced his accuracy of judgement, vital in battle. Here we have some interesting parallels in man's psyche.

Mars also has a special relationship with Venus. Married to the ugly Vulcan, she set up an adulterous relationship with the war god. This combination was delightful for a time but it caused Mars's humiliation before his fellow gods when Vulcan, by means of a fine, almost invisible net, tied the undiscerning lovers up for an Olympian exposé. This was a lesson for Mars as his sharp eye and swift action had been softened and dulled by Venus. Nezah had swamped Gevurah. Passion had blunted judgement and this temptation has sent more than just illicit lovers to the wall.

Mars' armour is very interesting. The function of these plates of metal and leather is to prevent hurt, to limit injury and protect the body. It does, however, constrict the wearer, set a clear boundary between the hard exterior and soft inner body. It is said by Kabbalists that Gevurah not only makes severe judgements, if not balanced by merciful Hesed, but over-confines the potent energy coming from the positive side of the Tree. Here the symbol of Mars acts like a control, as a para-military force does within a community under the law—Binah. Mars is at its best a good police force, at its worst the

Gestapo. In the human organism he represents all those processes that separate out the various substances and energies to where they are needed.

Mars is by its very name Martial, force under discipline, precise orders carried out without question, but it can only operate well under the restraint of something higher. The intelligent soldier hardly ever needs to use violence, though his actions must be decisive.

Of the planet Mars we know little except that its apparent movements are sudden and occasionally erratic, sometimes drawing remarkably close to the Earth, at others pulling right away, his red face just detected as an unflickering point. This is very much like day to day emotion and, while one should not parallel the analogue too closely, it is interesting that, next to Venus or Nezah, Mars is the closest planet to the Earth.

Jupiter occupies the position of Hesed on the Tree of Life. This is the point of expansion, of great energy before it is checked by Gevurah. Also attributed to this sefirah are the qualities of magnificence, magnanimity, mercy, all marks of Jupiter the beneficent god—though when uncontrolled, a danger with his endless largesse. This is shown very clearly in the round of myths connected with his loves. In these he pursues mortal women and goddesses to spread his vast reservoir of most potent seed, leading to numerous half-immortals and heroes. This is the particular power of Hesed. One story well illustrates the effect of undiluted magnificence. Semele, daughter of King Cadmus, asked to see her god-lover in all his glory. Jupiter attempted to dissuade her but in the end he gave in and she was blasted out of existence by his splendour like a snowflake in a furnace.

Jupiter was King on Olympus and about him circled the other gods. From the point of view of the Solar system this could be taken several ways. Whereas the Sun appears to be the pivot of the planetary organisation it may be, in fact, only a terminal pole with the planet Pluto at the outer end. Moreover, Jupiter not only lies roughly in the centre of the planetary chain stretching out from the Sun but it is the largest planet. This is more than significant because the size of Jupiter is the greatest a molecular body can be before the spontaneous generation of an atomic process can begin. The Sun is running down whereas there is reason to believe that Jupiter is growing. It already emits radio frequencies close to the Sun's. In addition to this, the king-sized planet has a full retinue of twelve satellites, some larger than our Moon. It is already a miniature Solar system, though this is mere interesting speculation.

*Figure 20—ASTROLOGY*

*This, as can be seen, is an integrated system based upon a set of laws that have the same origin as Kabbalah. The celestial bodies represent the various sefirot but in both their active and passive modes. Thus, while Mercury in Virgo is focused and reasoned, as the ruler of Gemini the planet is highly volatile and wide ranging. The triangles of the four elements echo the four Worlds that comprise Existence. The Fiery signs of Leo, Aries and Sagittarius radiate energy, in contrast to the Watery signs of Pisces, Cancer and Scorpio. These three correspond to the fluidic world of ever-changing forms. Various astrological combinations give rise to unique historic epochs and distinct periods in one's personal fate. (Cosmic Clock, design by Halevi).*

As a god, Jupiter generated many minor cults as well as children. Dionysius, one of his sons, was not only known for his exuberant festivals of wine but also for madness. Yet another example of excess use of bountiful power.

The position of Hesed on the Tree might well explain the negative aspect of Jupiter. Receiving the Lightning Flash of Divine energy from Binah, Jupiter also sits immediately below Hokhmah and takes in the pure vertical input of masculine energy from above. This sefirah, be it planet or person, if blocked will be charged with such a dynamic that there must be a release or explosion—hence Jupiter's profligacy—or in human terms genius and productivity. Van Gogh the painter is a good example. Driven by the unbalanced positive energy from Hokhmah and Hesed, he had to paint or go mad which he eventually did when he found it impossible to control the force passing through him. Dostoyevsky, the writer, as an epileptic had the same problem with his frenetic and prolific vision. Jupiter may seem at first sight all beneficent but the god was not always a pleasant despot. He carried a thunderbolt which he threw at unwary mortals and his aim was not always accurate. This wide-angled spray is characteristic of both Jupiter and Gedulah, or Greatness, another Hebrew name for Hesed. While dynamic proliferation, creation and magnanimity are needed, they must be disciplined by Gevurah. Perhaps this is why Jupiter could never really master his wife Hera, for all his power.

Moving back up the Tree along the Lightning Flash we pass through the invisible sefirah known as Daat—Knowledge—before we reach Binah, or Saturn in this planetary scheme. Some modern Kabbalists not only describe this transition point as the entry into what is known as the supernal triad of Keter, Hokhmah and Binah but ascribe this position to the planet Pluto. Now, while any thoughts on this idea may be at present hypothetical, they are very useful as a way of considering this intermediary sefirah.

The god Pluto was the brother of both Neptune and Jupiter. He was King of the Underworld or, to put it in Christian terms, the Outer Darkness—in an astronomical sense roughly Pluto's remote position in the Solar system. Moreover, he had a famous cap of invisibility. This could be read in two ways: that he was monarch of the dead, of those who have passed out of our dimension of sight, or that his processes are so slow (the planet has an orbital period of 247 years) that one lifetime is not enough to observe its full cycle. Pluto is the King of death, the planet of the most profound transformation man can physically witness. This event comes and goes, nothing can prevent it. Suddenly a being who has been a piece of human furniture in a society or family has vanished, disappeared into another world, the realm of shades. Hades' Gate may indeed be knowledge; for it is said that on death, everything learned is reviewed as the past life is rapidly uncoiled in an ecstatic flash of every pleasure, pain, ignorance and understanding lived. Here at the invisible door the experience and essence of a man is further distilled, the limiting ego evaporated for ever in the void of the divine Father and Mother before the final union with the Creator.

Pluto orbits at the very edge of the Solar system. Beyond lies the realm of the local star cluster and, containing this, the vast galactic arm of the Milky Way. Pluto's strange eccentric orbit is the margin and frontier of the planetary world and who knows what barrier or bridge this dark unseen planet describes?

The god Pluto was much feared on the surface of the Earth; but it must be remembered that his wife Persephone, a daughter of Earth, comes to the surface from the Underworld as Spring each year.

Pluto is certainly an unknown, both as a planet and a kabbalistic principle, but this we do know, that Daat is a point of profound transformation whether you are travelling up or down the Tree of Life.

The sefirah of Binah is filled by the god and planet Saturn. According to myth tradition, Saturn or Chronos (the Greek name) was one of the elder gods or Titans, Jupiter being his son who later displaced him as King. This appears to indicate a clear differentiation between the upper triad of Binah, Hokhmah, and Keter and the middle triad of Hesed, Gevurah, and Tiferet. Saturn, the god of form, is in the correct position on the Tree for it is the first passive principle, the cosmic Mother who changes the energy of Hokhmah into formulation. It is said that Saturn is the original Old Father Time. Time is the first limitation. Out of it unfolds change and change means the inter-relationship of energy and form. Saturn is also associated with those things that are old and proven. It is the conservative element at its worst and the perception of eternal principles at its best. In man Binah represents understanding, that is, the recognition of what is. This realisation takes perhaps three quarters of a life span. Old age is called the period of Saturn. Positively viewed, this phase is the era of contemplation at the closing of the circle of life. Repeating patterns are seen—the interweaving of events, the workings of fate and the ebb and flow of the forces of life and death. These things can only be revealed from a great distance, height or depth. Saturn is reputed to have just that viewpoint. He is perhaps the most philosophical of the gods, having experienced it all many times in his position as father of the King of Olympia. To him, in his orbit far outside Jupiter and the inner planets, all events are encompassed by his slower year. He has seen it all before.

Cast in the form of an old man, lean and bearded with a scythe, he is often associated with grimness and melancholy. This more commonplace image overlays an intelligent gravity, a mind that sees an overall plan. In this long vision Saturn is supreme. He can set out an idea, create a master design, knowing its results well beyond the time horizon of the other gods. From Binah or Saturn flows not only the received and passed-on divine impulse but a form, a set of principles, by which the Lightning Flash may manifest itself in the lower Worlds. This, in architectural terms, would be the layout of a new town. Buildings may come and go but the type of development, urban, market or manufacturing, will remain the same for a long time before it changes its basic scheme. This is Saturn, god of conservation as well as form.

Binah is sometimes known as the Mother because its passive role is embodied in Saturn. Saturn is resistant to change. The other planets rapidly alter their position relative to the Sun but he plods on, carrying his rings of limitation with him. These rings may be the product of an event occurring before organic life on Earth. They certainly indicate a major change of balance within the Solar system and this is mentioned in many world myths on the origin of the Universe. From the point of view of man, Saturn is the furthest planet that can be seen by the normal naked eye. Here, for ordinary man, the Solar system finishes. Telescopes may bring the image of the planet nearer but nothing else. This was, to the ancients, the limit beyond which little else was known or perceived except by speculation and illumination. At Binah this would appear to be correct for Hokhmah is almost as undefinable as Keter, whereas Binah at least has the first recognisable impressions of an outline. This is the essence of Saturn, the inception of Chronos — time and form.

The sefirah of Hokhmah is traditionally filled by the Zodiac. This is the band round the sky representing the path of the Sun. Besides enclosing the orbits of all the other planets, the Zodiac defines twelve phases of a continuous cosmic process. The idea is ancient and is embodied, on the level of man, in the twelve tribes of Israel and the

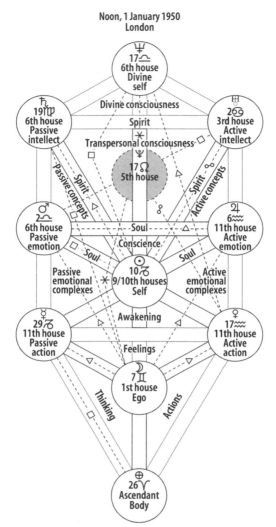

*Figure 21—HOROSCOPE*

*A birth chart is made for the moment of birth. This is when the fluidic psyche is crystallised into the physical body. This means that the temperament of an individual is fixed, to a degree. In this chart the position of the celestial bodies in the zodiac and what are called the mundane Houses are set out on the Tree with their geometric relationships. These stresses and eases give great insight into the person's fate as an indication of how they will behave in life. In this case, with Sun in Capricorn and Moon in Gemini, the Self will be prudent while the ego will be indiscreet if not under the Sun's (or Self's) control. This maybe the lesson the person has to learn in this particular incarnation. (Halevi).*

disciples of Christ. In this number all the human types were expressed, thus forming the complete circle of Mankind. In the realm of Nature, a similar process may be seen in the twelve phases of the natural year. For example the Sun, when in the sign of Taurus, is manifest in the Northern hemisphere of Earth as Spring, the time of courtship, mating, nest-building, growth and birth. Precisely opposite in the natural year lies Scorpio, the sign the Sun passes through in Autumn. Here we witness the falling of the leaves and drying out of cast-off fruit. The fields are brown and the summer birds have already flown. It is a time of decay, the beginning of the end of the natural cycle when the vital energies of life are spent. Everywhere there is the smell of rot and death—and yet within each fallen fruit lies a new seed, at the root of every shrivelled leaf is a new bud. Taurus and Scorpio are cosmic opposites: one the entry into physical life and the other the departure from it in physical death. Yet each contains at its heart the inner content of the other, both are a mirror in Nature of archetypal law—in this lies the essence of Hokhmah.

The Zodiac in Hokhmah contains all possibilities. The potential streaming out from this sefirah is enormous. Before it is received and contained by Binah, any combination is possible. The Zodiac describes twelve broad definitions but each one of these is full of variation in its own right. The potentiality summed up in the sign of Capricorn is vast. Here is stability and strength, order, hierarchy, patience and time. In Aries we have the dynamic of initiative, originality, courage, skill, sacrifice and vision—and these are mere human manifestations of these root principles! Multiplied by twelve, plus the several levels at which these archetypes operate, we have the full range from which a particular Tree of Life may develop, be it a man or the twelve Olympians.

At this point we may see how the emanations streaming out from Keter are changed, by passing through each sefirah, until they reach their final form in Malkhut. From the conversion into actual potential by the action of Hokhmah, the emanations are formulated into major principles by Binah. These are developed and expanded within their context by Hesed, then refined by the discrimination of Gevurah into the recognisable entity of Tiferet. Nezah then sets the thing working while Hod relates it to the outside world. Yesod maintains its balance and gives it a view of itself. Malkhut is what we see in its physical form when the Tree is complete, having brought the creative process down to Earth.

Some modern Kabbalists insert the planet Uranus in the sefirah of Hokhmah. Though not universally agreed on, the notion contains some interesting ideas. Uranus was the father of Saturn, who dethroned him early on in the making of the Universe. Uranus was the son of Gaea, the primal Mother Goddess, appearing after Chaos at the beginning of Creation. Uranus was her first son. From their relationship came Saturn, her last born, who rendered his father impotent and then was, in time, dethroned by Jupiter his own son.

Apart from a certain vague parallel with the Bible, perhaps more interesting is the fact that Uranus is the god of the starry cosmos—the seed bed of the Zodiac. He was also considered by the Greeks as a primordial divinity and who, together with his mother, were considered the grandparents of the world. While not corresponding precisely with the Tree of Life there is nevertheless some interesting material to be thought about—and with any study of Kabbalah the process never finishes. As in life, crystallisation means atrophy and death.

Modern Kabbalists, as in the case of Hokhmah and Daat, ascribe for teaching purposes a god and planet to Keter. This is Neptune, brother of Jupiter and God of the Sea. As powerful as Jupiter, he took up the rulership of the middle world of water with Jupiter above in the sky and Pluto below in the underworld. As a symbol of his power he carried a trident, perhaps a key to the three divine forces or trinity which go to create the Universe. Another quality of Neptune is that, like the sea, he is omnipotent, like the presence of water all over the Earth. Some Kabbalists see this as significant and speculate on the flowing nature of his being, referring to the fact that he is the older brother to Jupiter. These ideas, however, are only fragments of a larger pattern, now lost, and are probably distorted by time.

Traditionally the sefirah of Keter is described on this scale as the *Primum Mobile*—the Prime Mover. This name is more or less self-explanatory. But what moves, and who moves it, is another matter, for it is more than an unseen sphere singing as it rotates the seven heavens. Embedded in the idea of the *Primum Mobile* is the same concept as in Keter—the Crown. What streams through the Crown from above is identical to that which lies beyond the *Primum Mobile*. Perhaps it is pertinent to say at this point that above the planetary, and above even the Prime Mover on this scale, lie three other Universes in all. This accords with the kabbalistic idea, dealt with in the next chapter, that there are four Trees of Life, each one part of a vast chain stretching from the Divine Universe, through the Worlds of Creation and

Formation to the realm of elements and action—the one in which we live. On this scale the scheme we have been examining is in fact the lowest and densest universe and the planets observed in the sky are the tiny hard physical cores of vast organisations. We see the Sun as a brilliant ball but, in reality, we live inside its radiant body as we do within the outer Van Allen radiation belt and atmosphere of Earth. Our planet does not cease to be until well beyond the Moon. If we could view it with cosmic eyes, it would take the form of a vast pulsating tadpole with its diaphanous tail blown back by Solar winds, rather than a solid and small blue and green sphere. This is the World of Asiyyah—the elements and action, the final stage of Keter when, at the end of the creative process, it becomes Malkhut.

Here then is the Tree of Life laid out in terms of the old gods and the ideas they symbolised. By combining this with the corresponding knowledge and experience of the sefirot present in oneself, yet more insight into their nature can be gained. This is the practical application of the 'As above so below' principle so often quoted in ancient philosophy.

72

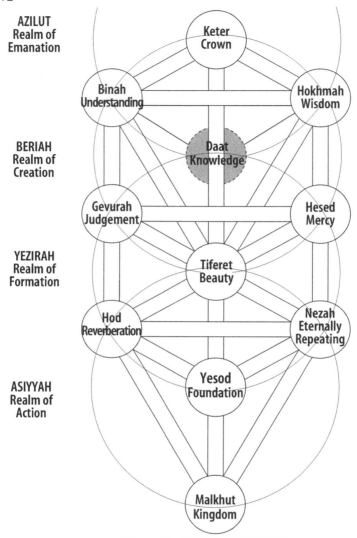

AZILUT
Realm of
Emanation

BERIAH
Realm of
Creation

YEZIRAH
Realm of
Formation

ASIYYAH
Realm of
Action

Keter
Crown

Binah
Understanding

Hokhmah
Wisdom

Daat
Knowledge

Gevurah
Judgement

Hesed
Mercy

Tiferet
Beauty

Hod
Reverberation

Nezah
Eternally
Repeating

Yesod
Foundation

Malkhut
Kingdom

*Figure 22—FOUR POTENTIALS*
*Within the first Divine Tree are the seeds of all that will come into being. Here the four Worlds are inherent in the Tree's structure. At the top is the Radiance of the Divine Fire. Out of this is emanates the possibility of Creation or the Airy universe of the Spirit. Emerging from this process comes the Watery World of Formation, from which the Earthy domain of physicality will eventually come. Together they are what was, now is, and what will be as long as the Holy One wills it. Should the Absolute withdraw, the wish to manifest the universe would vanish into No-thing-ness again. (Halevi).*

# 6. The Four Worlds

Having set out the nature of the sefirot we pause, before exploring their relationships, to see how they fit into a yet grander design.

As there are four states of matter in the physical World—fire, air, water, and earth—so there are four corresponding levels within the relative Universe. Traditionally these are known as Azilut or the World of Emanation, Beriah or the World of Creation, Yezirah, the World of Formation and Asiyyah, the World of Substance and Action. These four realms form a chain of increasing density and number of laws the further they are removed from the Azilutic World. Each level is a fainter mirror of the one above until in the Asiyyatic World—the one we exist in—the materiality is so dense that we often only observe the surface of our environment.

In the great Tree of Life that composes all Creation these four Worlds are set out in the general major horizontal divisions of the Keter, Hokhmah and Binah triad (Azilut); the upper square formed by Hokhmah, Binah, Gevurah and Hesed (Beriah); the lower square constructed by Hesed, Gevurah, Nezah and Hod with Tiferet at its centre (Yezirah); and the lower triad made up of Nezah, Hod and Malkhut with Yesod at its centre (Asiyyah). Beginning at the top triad, these horizontal divisions roughly correspond to the four Worlds. I say roughly because it is also in the nature of these Worlds to interpenetrate each other, not only on the Tree but literally, as heat does air, air water, and water, earth.

Kabbalists see the relationship between the Worlds on the Tree in various ways. Some see the demarcation in the horizontal while others see it in the central triangles. Some, for instance, take Tiferet as the lowest point of the Beriatic World, with Yesod performing the same rôle for the World of Yezirah as it penetrates the Asiyyatic triangle.

This idea of the four Universes is carried further in the notion that each World has its own complete Tree, so that the Malkhut of the Tree of the Azilutic World is the Tiferet of Beriah, interleaving down to the bottom-most Malkhut where the residue of all the Worlds is concentrated. This idea follows the rule that every complete unit in the Universe is based on the Tree. Moreover, it is said that within these miniature Trees the four Worlds are repeated and so on down to the smallest complete cosmos. This is quite different from the fact that within each individual sefirah there is another complete sub-Tree.

In man these four Worlds correspond to different levels of his being. The lowest triad is the physical body, the lower square the realm of emotion while the upper square matches the intellect. The topmost triad relates to the Divine. Various traditions have other names like carnal, subtle, rational and Divine bodies but the meanings are much the same.

It is useful to identify these levels within oneself and one can easily observe them in any creative process or full human relationship. For instance, in a love affair it sometimes becomes quickly apparent as to what is or is not there in head, heart and gut. The predominance of one, or absence of another, quickly reveals itself. When all four are balanced the miraculous occurs.

Taking the World of Azilut first this can be described, if at all, as the realm in which the Tree of Life is in its purest state. It is indeed functioning in the realm of emanations. Here, close to the Endless Light, all the sefirot are radiations or resonances directly in contact with the Divine.

Traditionally the sefirot are called by various God names, each one the purest aspect of the Absolute as manifest in the relative Universe. From our distant view very little is known about them and to pretend to this knowledge would be foolish. Mystical experiences are well known to be indescribable, not because of the lack of articulation on the part of the participants but because there is no language or symbol adequate for illustration. It could be said to be like explaining Einstein's energy-mass equation to a sheep.

For those deeply interested in these names of power, as they are called, there is a great deal of literature. But this study does not require books while to make contact with a master of the art is remote for anyone who has not been under practical discipline for some time. Therefore I would suggest that at this point we follow the brief set in this book and observe the Tree of Life primarily at the Asiyyatic and perhaps the Yeziratic level.

The Beriatic World, the realm of Creation, is said to be of the Universe of Archangels. These might be defined as intelligences that are concerned with the implementing of Divine instruction and which

*Figure 23—FOUR REALITIES*

*Ezekiel the prophet beheld a vision of the four universes. In ancient times symbolism was the language of knowledge that contained metaphysical ideas. Here the priestly mystic views, from the lowest, natural World, the Chariot of the angelic realm and its cycles. Kabbalists regarded the planets as angels, whose essences were rooted in the astral World of Formation, while the Sun was seen as a minor archangelic being which decorated the Throne of Heaven. Upon this great seat sat the illuminating figure of Adam Kadmon, also called the* Kavod, *the Glory of God.* (The Bear Bible, 16th century).

set in motion the designing processes. At this level nothing may be seen, like the concept of a building long before even the sketch plans have been drawn. Here myriads of possibilities may be inherent. Out of one idea a new type of architecture may spring. This is the moment of creative activity before the formulation phase is set.

The Tree in the Beriatic Universe would describe the same operations as in the lower Worlds but the level of energy and density would be of greater potency. The Malkhut of Beriah contains elemental qualities that would make our most creative works crude and infantile.

The Yeziratic World is closer to our understanding. It is the realm of forms. Here the creative process is fluid and developing, like soft potters' clay while it is being worked.

At this point subtlety manifests, endless variation and variety are possible but within the context set up in the Beriatic World. Here moulds are made and filled, changed and reformed. Here an ebb and flow occurs, configurations emerge and dissolve as they continually meet the requirements of a set of conditions. Yet always everything relates to the original concept. Many of man's arts are peepholes into the Yeziratic World and his pursuit, for instance, of symbolism is an attempt to fix this strange realm in Asiyyatic terms.

The Asiyyatic realm is composed of the elements. It is literally the World in which we live. However, it is not quite as simple as pure physics, for the upper Worlds permeate it. A cat originates from a thought in the mind of Nature in order to fulfill a cosmic need, as did the dinosaurs and as men do now. From this view one cat is all cats and all cats are but copies of one cat. Here we have a creative impulse originating in the Beriatic World and being manifested through its changing kitten, cat, corpse form in the Asiyyatic World. If we ask the question, 'What is a cat?' in the Asiyyatic World, it is but the rearrangement of several hundred tins of cat food plus air, water and light. Solid as pussy may be, she is not what she seems; nor are any of us in the Asiyyatic World.

So familiar are we with the phenomena of this realm that we tend to consider it as if it were the only one. The physical Universe, however cosmic it may appear, is only the face of the upper Worlds though in its reality it contains them all.

In the realm of Nature we see the ever-changing forms of flora and fauna. Here the elements move through an endless cycle only for a moment frozen in this or that plant or animal. But consider the construction of the millions of leaves in an orchard, and the original printed circuit for the exchange of energies needed, with the slow modification by mutation going on as the climate of the planet alters from ice to tropical age. All this is going on while men charge the atmosphere with radio waves and with thoughts and feelings, not to mention the accumulation of the residue of generations of lives.

Above the World of Nature is the planet and, beyond this, the other planets, the Sun and the local star clusters. All these, including the Milky Way that we see stretched across the heavens on a clear night, are the World of Asiyyah. When we look up or down we see matter and however slowly a galaxy may turn in comparison to our reference to time it is still in the realm of elements. Even the smallest atom belongs to the Asiyyatic World, though its energy aspect may fall into the upper portion of the Asiyyatic Tree of Life.

Man lives in the Asiyyatic World. He does, however, have access to the upper Universes should he evolve and refine his being to be able to become aware of these realms. In order to do this he has to acquire more than the physical body Nature has supplied. He must organise out of the substances and energies permeating his being a new vehicle for each World. This takes time and work, knowledge and practice. It is said that this is man's unique position. He can evolve as an individual. He has the possibility of rising above the gradual evolution of all creation and to surpass the angels and archangels who, though of an initially higher order of intelligence, are fixed in their roles and function in the Cosmic Pattern. Man alone can by-pass the left and right sides of the Tree of Life and go straight up the middle column.

Looked at as a whole, the four Worlds may be seen as four concentric bands, Azilut on the outer ring, Asiyyah at the centre, each with ten ring divisions representing the ten sefirot of each World, centred on the pivot of Malkhut within the Asiyyatic Circle. Beyond the outer periphery of the Keter of the Azilutic World is the circumference of the Endless Light and beyond this the other two veils of negative existence enclosed by the Absolute. Within the outer ring of the Azilutic Keter the density increases each step inwards, the outmost ring or sefirah containing all the ones inside. In this way every link in this cosmic chain is ruled from above while controlling those below. In terms of the density of vibrations, the cyclic rates appear to increase the nearer to the centre we go or the lower we descend; though in fact the subtler rates are present but undetectable in, say, the Asiyyatic Universe. This interpenetration of the higher Worlds into the lower might explain many things about the so-called 'next world', miracles and other supernatural phenomena.

*Figure 24—FOUR BODIES*
*According to instructions given to Moses, the vestments of the High Priest were to*
*represent different levels within a human being. The headdress and top coat symbolised*
*the Divine over the garment that was equated with the Spirit. Beneath this was the*
*chequered raiment of the soul which signified the choice between good and evil. The*
*priest's body was related to the Earth or the material World. His posture indicated the*
*three pillars of the Tree of Life with the Holy Name of God inscribed upon the*
*headband. The twelve symbols hung about his brow represented the tribes of Israel*
*or zodiacal types of humanity. (Drawing by Halevi).*

The different levels defined in this circular scheme of the four Worlds were laid out by the Kabbalists, at one point, into an evolutionary ladder called the Fifty Gates. This describes the progressive stages from Chaos, through the formation of the elements, to the Earth as we know it. It then proceeds to unfold the story of the rise of the vegetable kingdom out of the mineral world, then of animal life up to the vertebrate. Next the evolution of man is shown with the step-by-step growth of his completion in the image of God. This is followed by a description of the heavenly spheres, from the Moon up through the planetary levels to the Empyrean Heaven beyond the *Primum Mobile*. After this the angelic levels of the celestial hierarchies are laid out with the last gate at the portal of Ayin Sof, the Endless Light.

These cosmographs may seem quaint to us in modern terms but it is perhaps more a question of language than accuracy. An angel, defined as a Cherubim, was quite different in nature and function from a Seraphim. This was in medieval times as precise a vocabulary as any in modern physics, perhaps more so. To us the symbolism may have no obvious meaning in our experience or perhaps we call the same things by different names. However, the important thing to remember is that this scheme of the Universe was based on the same principles as the Tree. For some it was speculation, for others a working hypothesis and for others perhaps a world either in imagination or reality. The same arguments apply to modern atomic physics and astronomy.

One final point. The Kabbalist also sets out a mirror arrangement called the Kellippot. This was the realm of demons or the world of shells. Caused by distortion, imbalance and atrophy, these were corresponding forces on every level of the Universe but out of line with general evolution. Any organisation has these present and they manifest when excess is reached either in over-activity or over-resistance. The symbol of shells indicates their fixity, their stop of flow, their separation from the living body. Thus, in human terms, a man who has lost contact with his humanity may become an officer in a Nazi concentration camp—a very demon! Similarly a country in civil war (the worst kind of war) is literally beset by arch-demons, though we call them the forces of Communism or Fascism. The bitter Thirty Years War between Catholic and Protestant Europe illustrates how religious powers can become demonic. For different reasons a Kellippotic situation occurs when a country, or a man, stagnates in development. Historic inertia or traditional violence solidify into a rigid custom in a community, preventing economic growth or human rights, while corruption is tolerated. In a man such a hard psychological shell of lethargy or over-activity can strangle his personal evolution and so prevent him from ever seeing the world outside his own fixed image of it.

All Kellippotic phenomena signify the disturbance of the natural interplay of the sefirot. The lack of or over-stimulus of the active or passive processes can create an imbalanced situation to a greater or lesser degree. Any permanent distortion in a Tree will generate a disastrous circumstance: on a large scale, global war, on the individual level, madness—indeed possession by devils.

Here then are the four Worlds and the four horizontal divisions of the Tree of Life. As said, for the purpose of this study we will mostly concentrate on the Asiyyatic world, so that by observing its working on our level we can perhaps glimpse into the upper Worlds.

# 7. *Triad and Octave*

It is said that the relative Universe comes into existence through the interaction of two great laws. The first is the Law of the Triad Trinity which brings about an event and the second is the Law of Octaves which shows the development of that event through a definite sequence. Both these laws are present everywhere, from the inception of Divine Creation down to the commonplace action of the striking of a match. Nothing can exist outside these two laws.

The concept of the Trinity is familiar in most major religions and philosophies and Kabbalah is no exception. In the Tree of Life it is seen very precisely in the triad Keter, Hokhmah, and Binah. Here are the positive and negative factors shown in the pillars of force and form, with the third element of equilibrium bringing them into relationship in the central column. Nothing can happen until all three are in relationship, no more than a child can be conceived without the various conditions being right between a man and a woman. So it is throughout the Universe, wherever a real event occurs.

It will be noted on looking at the Tree that all the sefirot form themselves into triads. Moreover, every one of these triads is connected with the central column of consciousness. This is vital for, while the left and right columns are fixed in function (in the same way that a man is a man and nothing else), the central column completes any triad, thus enabling events to flow. It will also be observed that there are great triads and small triads in the Tree and particular triads that relate principally to the central axis. All these have their special place in the cosmic scheme of the Tree and most may behave in any one of six permutations which range through growth, decay, transformation, disease, renewal, and regeneration.

The Law of Octaves is based on the idea that between Keter and Malkhut stretches a great string, a monochord, with the note Do at the top and bottom of the axis of consciousness. Here is another insight into the kabbalistic saying that 'Keter is in Malkhut and Malkhut is in Keter'. From the view that this is a vast vibrating string, we may see

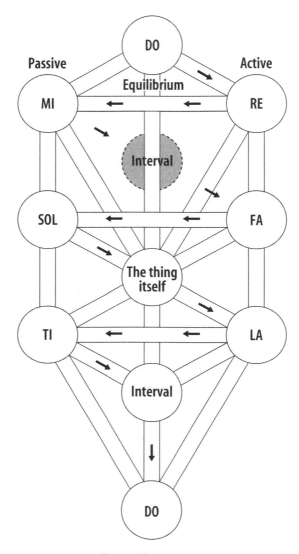

*Figure 25—OCTAVE*

*One of the major laws of Existence is that of the Octave. It follows the Lightning Flash of emanation down but it also defines the zigzag path of ascent. This movement between pillars allows for growth and decay, expansion and contraction and many other operations vital to manifestation and evolution. The two intervals are crucial points in any process. They mark a pause in which a change of direction can occur. Without these two junctions, Existence would be no more than a cosmic machine without any possibility of variation. (Halevi).*

that all other vibrations in the Universe are contained in this monochord; though they, however many, cannot compose it, any more than a billion people are a complete Adam. This monochord is of quite a different order. It is the Master Octave while all the others are minor and mere harmonies to its great notes.

Like Jacob's Ladder with the angels ascending and descending, the Octave has two main movements, up and down. In music we see the principle of the notes becoming higher and of greater frequency as we move from Do, through Re, Mi, Fa, Sol, La, Ti to Do. This is because the string is being shortened and so more vibrations are being packed into a smaller pitch or space. In the Universe this takes on a great deal of meaning when we consider the wave and particle theories. As we descend towards the lower end of matter, density increases, that is, more particles are packed into a smaller space. Likewise when we look at vibrations—and these are interchangeable with the particles of matter—these appear to increase also, though not in the sense that we usually understand high frequency. For it must be recalled that more beats imply a shortening of the string, bringing greater tension but less flexibility. Here is a situation the converse of our normal perception of increased frequency, for in fact any phenomenon in a high vibration zone is under a greater constriction or more laws. The infinitesimal motions and periods of atoms, as against the slower but more flexible cell, describes very precisely the true situation of a materiality, where vibration is so compacted that nothing appears to move. I repeat, appears, for what we normally think about high vibration is that it is more powerful and free. As often said, appearances can be deceptive and in the real Universe often the reverse of what we see is the case. It is not without reason that man is sometimes viewed symbolically as contemplating the World upside down, seeing the transient as eternal and the eternal as transient. This is the first veil of illusion we live in.

If we consider the Tree of Life in this light we shall observe that the bottom Do of our usual view in fact starts at the top, at Keter, and resolves in its maximum vibration and compression in Malkhut. To baffle us further the Octave flows two ways, unwinding its intensity into the great monochord of Keter having passed through the frets of the sefirot. Both these flows occur simultaneously like a two-way lightning flash joining Heaven and Earth in a single impulse which, in turn, contains all the impulses of every level, high or low, down to the minutest movements of the atoms of the densest metal. This is the raising of the Kingdom up to the Crown and the bringing of the

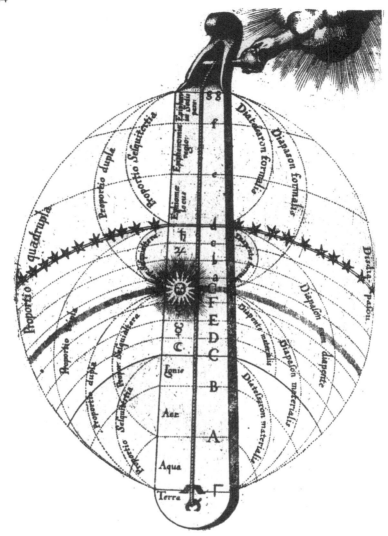

*Figure 26—CELESTIAL MUSIC*
*In this 17th century engraving an English Kabbalist set out here to present Existence*
*as a system of harmonies based upon the notion of the music of the spheres. Modern*
*science has discovered that the Law of Octaves governs the electromagnetic spectrum*
*and the way the material world is organised. There is the question as to how the*
*ancients could make their discoveries about these subtle laws without scientific*
*instruments. The answer is that the mystics themselves were, with the eye of imagination,*
*the microscopes and telescopes of their time, because a human being is a microcosm*
*of Existence.* (Robert Fludd).

Crown down to the Kingdom, so that Heaven may manifest in Earth. The Law of Octaves, besides being seen in the one great progression from Keter to Malkhut, can be observed on every scale, including quite mundane phenomena such as the light spectrum, the periodic table of elements and of course as music. Using the familiar tonal scale, but remembering to reverse the apparent increase and decrease of frequency, we can plot the nature of the Octave's development, when related to the Tree of Life.

Striking the seemingly lower but in fact greater Do of Keter the Octave moves down the path of the Lightning Flash to Hokhmah. Here, in its first manifestation, it enters the world of vibration at its initial fret or stop. Energy is now present. It then crosses to Binah, the second note, where in the first passive sefirah it is slowed further and becomes locked in form, however rarefied it may appear to us. This is the first triad. From here, after an interval which we shall deal with in a moment, it flows on down through the sefirot of the Tree. It does not, however, appear directly to touch the central column again until it reaches the Do of Malkhut. The reason for this is the peculiar law that determines Octaves.

After the supernal triad of Keter, Hokhmah, and Binah has set creation in motion there is a momentary pause, a slowing down that has to be bridged. This phenomenon is observable in any creative work in ordinary life when there is an initial hesitance after a vigorous start. If this gap is not crossed, the action stops. Many books and pictures, well begun, have died at this critical point. What is needed is an impulse from outside to carry the movement over. In minor tasks often a walk, a conversation or a coffee act as the necessary stimulus. This boost takes the flow across to the note Fa or the sefirah Hesed, the vital gap being filled by the invisible sefirah Daat which supplies the contact with the central column of conscious energy.

The Octave continues down the Lightning Flash following the development of the various sefirot, through Fa (Hesed), Sol (Gevurah) to La (Nezah). Here again it has traversed the central column of equilibrium. By this time it has become apparent what the character of the Octave is and this nature is embodied in Tiferet. Anyone practising creative work knows that once this point has been reached there is no changing. The essence of the book or picture is fixed. Only by beginning anew can any major discrepancy be corrected. Here again the third force—that of consciousness—manifests but this time as the image of all the steps of the Octave that have occurred and will

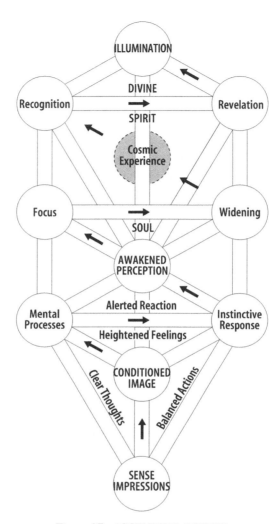

*Figure 27—ASCENDING OCTAVE*
*In this Tree we see how an individual, upon seeing Jerusalem for the first time, might have a moment of enlightenment. First they sense the sights, sounds and smells of the city in a normal way. Initially this would only register as a preconditioned image based upon their cultural background. However, upon recognising the city's profound significance, the ordinary mind would become alert as the soul triad was awakened. This would sharpen a deeper perception of Jerusalem's history and importance to three religions. Out of this might come, if they were a Kabbalist, the vision of Abraham's initiation by Melchizedek that took place on this spot before layer upon layer of history hid the connection between the Earthly and Heavenly Jerusalem. (Halevi).*

occur after; for the path is now already set and the result, except for details, crystallised. This is because all the paths feeding into Tiferet are now firmly focused.

After the nature of the Octave has been determined the sequence continues, on through La (Nezah–cycles) to Ti (Hod–reverberation). Then it comes to the last interval before completion. Here again this pause, often seen as heightened fatigue, is observable in quite ordinary tasks. A final major effort is needed to finish the sequence off. During the Second World War the British recognised this law at work in their war effort and the BBC put out two programmes of stimulating music at the times when it was known the factory workers were flagging. This may be a crude example but it was a practical understanding of the working-day Octave. In the case of the Tree this interval is filled by Yesod, the potent sefirah on the column of equilibrium. This vital centre completes three sub-triads in the big bottom triad of the Asiyyatic (action and matter) World thereby bringing the whole Octave into full physical manifestation. In a book, this is the final labour of actually setting words down and maintaining the flow over many weeks (no mean effort when it would be so easy just to think or talk about it). In Malkhut the final Do completes the process.

It might be well to repeat here that between every note of an octave is a miniature octave or, to put it in kabbalistic terms, there is a complete Tree in and between each sefirah. This often accounts for why we cannot see the law clearly, for we only observe at most times particular notes or sefirot. This could be because we have access to perhaps only one part in a complete process, like an editor who performs the Gevurah-Hod tasks of the publishing sequence. Another example would be in the Law Courts where we only see the Gevurah-Binah function of the legal system.

The interaction of the two great laws of Octave and Trinity is manifold and gives rise to the many aspects of the Universe. In man their interaction is well demonstrated and a trained eye can spot them at work. However, before we do our examination of the triads in relation to man, we must take note of certain subsidiary laws.

While in general the male column may be taken as the active principle flowing down into Yesod and Malkhut and the female column as the passive principle likewise joining there, it must be remembered the individual sefirot are subject to transvestism, that is, changing from negative to positive and *vice versa*. This is because of the fact that as the Lightning Flash descends, the upper sefirah always acts as the active principle to the recipient lower one in the flow of emanations. For example, Hesed is passive in relation to Binah and Gevurah, normally passive, is active in this circumstance in relation to Tiferet. Moreover, in each triad any one of the sefirot may take up an active, passive or neutral status within a limited situation, that is, when operating in a minor role. This may or may not work in balance to the whole Tree. Such a malfunction in man, for instance, is when a sefirah which should be active is passive or acting as the connecter. A good example of a passive sefirah usurping an active role is in the man who cannot get to sleep because his Hod cannot solve a problem outside its scope. The ordinary logical mind, becoming the active principle in the Hod, Yesod and Malkhut triad, runs the question round and round in an endless loop drawing on data stored in the brain which is seen as old and useless information on the Yesodic screen, offering no solution. Meanwhile, in his restlessness the vitality level in the Nezah-Yesod-Malkhut triad is dropping and quite unable to refresh the man because Nezah is rendered passive. The result is that there is not enough energy input from the active column of the Tree to lift him out of his locked situation. Eventually he falls asleep from sheer exhaustion. However, perhaps during the night when the Tree is functioning normally, his Gevurah judgement can come into operation. If not the night's rest, with Nezah performing naturally, will produce enough power in the organism to enable the man to tackle the problem in a balanced way next morning. Occasionally, as we all experience, solutions are produced by the upper sefirot during sleep while the lower triads replenish the body and excrete waste mind matter through dreams. For the most part all the triads work well within a normal range of permutations checking and counterbalancing each other throughout the Tree and these will be discussed later in detail after a general outline.

Taking the side triads first, these by their relationship to the force and form columns of the Tree are less flexible than those centred on the middle pillar. This is because the active and passive columns are more concerned with function than consciousness and therefore have less freedom of action. This is easily spotted in a person who always makes value judgements (excess Gevurah) or someone who has no self-discipline (lack of Gevurah). However, these functions do have important jobs to perform. To take examples in man, the Hod-Yesod-Malkhut triad defines the identifying processes, the memory and the body. Here is a continuous sequence of comparison. A story will illustrate some of the lower triads at work. While walking down the street a man's Hod is endlessly sorting out incoming impressions. He avoids a lamp-post, reads a poster, negotiates crossing the street between three fast-moving cars, using conditioned reflex experience stored up in his Hod-Yesod-Malkhut triad. He knows where he is going because, over the years, he has built up a picture of the district in this same triad which can draw on the memory bank in the brain and flash a plan on his Yesodic screen at will. However, he sees an unfamiliar alleyway and his Hod mind, ever-curious, directs his voluntary system to point his feet in that direction. On the other side of the Tree his Nezah-Yesod-Malkhut triad tells him that he is hungry, that he ought to go home and eat. His Hod mind, intrigued by the new sights, smells and sounds, ignores his hunger and prods him on. In the dim alleyway, on unfamiliar ground, his Nezah-Yesod-Malkhut triad adds a little adrenaline to his bloodstream. Already nervous, yet more stimulus is added by his Yesodic imagination as he takes on the fantasy role of a secret agent. Brave, good looking and determined he presses on, feeling the make-believe pistol hard against his throbbing chest. Turning a corner his Hod-informed eyes dilate as he sees the silhouette of a girl standing in the shadows. Totally immersed in his illusion, his Yesod fills in the unseen face with idealised features while his Nezah flushes a tinge of desire through his system. With his Hod-Nezah-Yesod triad suddenly excited, his sensual faculties are alert and his instincts expectant he approaches the girl half believing he will actually kiss her full and beautiful mouth. She turns abruptly and her face catches the light. It is old, hard, her lips are thin and dried. The Yesodic image vanishes, his Nezah is repulsed and his Hod quickly moves his Malkhut body past her. The whole dream evaporates into reality. Realising that he is a fool he hurries on, groping his way back to familiar ground where after the momentary Self-consciousness he once more drifts back into a Yesodic dream, this time about what he is to have for lunch, as his Nezahian hunger asks his Hod to guide his Malkhut feet, with Yesod's help, home.

Taking a perhaps more serious line we leave these lower triads and examine those attached higher up the central column. Here taking again the example of man, we set out the traditional triads going up the pillar of consciousness.

Man is only half a creature of the Earth. While living on the planet he is only partially under its laws. We read in the Bible that after his fall he was ejected from the Garden of Eden into the world below.

Here he was clothed in animal skins and on death was to be returned to the dust of which he was made.

These are very interesting statements on man's origin and composition, especially when set out on the Tree of Life upon which we are told he is modelled after his Maker's image. Firstly his body is literally made up of dust or earth. It contains the vital fluids, uses air and cannot live without heat or light. These are the elements as defined in Malkhut. He is also alive in an organic form. In him are all the processes of the vegetable world. He eats, drinks and breathes. He also grows and reproduces himself just as plants do. However, he is also an animal, with all the qualities of that realm. This makes him mobile, social, aggressive and loving, as well as many other attributes that are purely animal in their nature. The ideal family, with every activity from the cradle through childhood, courtship, marriage, home-making, career, to old age and the grave, are all part of the animal kingdom in man. Neither good nor bad, this is often seen as the human aspect of life when it is not. The human element of a man is that he is conscious of himself and knows that he is conscious. In this way he belongs to a very different kingdom from the animals.

The Tree defines the mineral level in Malkhut and the vegetable part of man in the great Hod-Nezah-Malkhut triad. Here are all the bodily processes and circulations with the vegetable intelligence centred on the Hod-Nezah-Yesod triad. In this small trinity the cyclic processes are governed, from the responses to the outer world through Hod to the inner repeating mechanisms of Nezah. Yesod is the sex act or pollination. The Hod-Nezah-Yesod triad can also be called the 'Flesh', that is, it bears Life, as against a corpse.

The triad Hod-Nezah-Tiferet is the animal soul, or *Nefesh* in traditional Hebrew, which refers to blood or Life. This animates the body, gives it a higher level of consciousness even to the point that it knows it exists but not that it knows that it knows. A cat is a very intelligent animal but it is blind and deaf to anything outside its own sense of life. It may be curious about strange objects or creatures but they play no part in its cat universe. It soon loses interest even in its own reflection and ceases to see it any more. Cats appear to have dreams, as any cat owner will tell you. A cat undoubtedly possesses a Yesod and growls and whines at the images the Hod-Nezah-Yesod triad circulates after a bad night with the local cat Mafia.

The Nefesh or animal soul is by no means as inferior as implied. It has direct contact with Tiferet and is the next stage up on the vertical axis of consciousness. The complex made up of Tiferet, Hod, Nezah, Yesod and Malkhut is a highly sophisticated organism with a clear identity, though not necessarily to itself. A tiger is a distinct species, as is a cow. They are individualised examples of this configuration. However, a man is more than a species because he contains the ability to develop the whole Tree. This is possible by the next triad Tiferet-Gevurah-Hesed which defines a man's self-awareness. In Hebrew this is known to some Kabbalists as *Ruah* which is 'breath' or 'wind'. This no doubt refers to God breathing life into Adam. However, study of the oldest Text, the Bible in Hebrew (Gen II:7), reveals that the term *Neshamah*, or living human soul, is used which is not of the same order as the animal and vegetable kingdoms. It is said that from the conception of a child to its birth the embryo passes through all the stages of natural evolution. Indeed it does for it forms, out of the elements coming into the mother's body, a growing organism like a plant. It then transforms into a sea animal swimming in the womb fluids before taking its first breath as a mammal. At what exact moment the human soul enters is still to be agreed though it is probably at the Tiferet point. It may be said, however, that a man's body at birth only contains genetic characteristics (the DNA molecules in the cells carrying out the brief set by the chromosomes) but these are confined to the race and family of the man, not his psyche. If this were not true there would be no variety in any family. It is the Neshamah that makes a man an individual. It is his self-consciousness that separates him from the animal and from most of his fellow men who tend to conform with tribal (social-animal) practices and customs. The Neshamah makes individuation possible, because of its link with Gevurah (Judgement) and Hesed (Mercy). Here are emotional, human faculties; animals have no judgement or mercy. They do not kill their own species in conflict because of Nezah and the intelligence of Nature which wishes to preserve the species. It is only highly-developed animals such as apes or well-organised societies like ants that fight. This may be due, in apes, to the arising of the beginning of self-consciousness and in ants to the fact that their society has mass intelligence greater than the individual ant. This is an area for study.

The Neshamah or soul, as we may also call it, pivoted on Tiferet has also access upwards to Keter. This gives it a unique point of reference and influx of power. Any man truly in contact and centred in Tiferet is indeed Self-conscious, for nearly all the paths focus there, though in ordinary men the upper ones may be just potential lines of communication.

The Bible implies in Gen I:2 that the triad formed by Hokhmah-Binah-Tiferet is the Ruah, the Breath or Spirit. Connected with the Divine triad this triangle, pivoted in Tiferet, may be called objective consciousness, that is, awareness of more than everything connected with one's self. Here is insight into the nature of the Universe. Things are seen not in a self-oriented way but in cosmic terms, larger than one's self however noble or pure it may be. Rooted in Binah (Understanding) and Hokhmah (Wisdom), how else could it view creation? Moreover it interfaces with the divine triad of Binah-Hokhmah-Keter. This gives it a direct relationship with the Divine World, the Azilutic Universe of emanations. It is said by the Kabbalists that at death the Malkhut body returns to the elements, Yesod soon separating out as the vegetable processes cease. The Neshamah retreats into the World of the psyche while the Spirit withdraws to the World of Creation. However, the soul and the spirit remain interconnected.

The topmost triad is the Supernal Trinity. This is the Divine World in man and Creation. From here streams the three forces of the Trinity and the flowing sequences of the Octaves and sefirot. The Kabbalists further defined the central triads into two main complexes. The upper one was known as the great or long face and this was composed by the Keter-Hokhmah-Binah-Tiferet form. Here the face and beard of God reaches down through the Universe, each hair carrying its divine instruction and existence. The lower face was composed of Tiferet, Hod, Nezah and Malkhut. This was called the lower face or lesser assembly. Here is Adam or mankind.

# 8. Paths

The basic statement of the Tree of Life is that all is one, though there may appear to be many aspects, principles and processes involved. From this it could be said that the Tree is a nuclear cell which divides up into the ten sefirot, through which flow the Divine Emanations setting in motion the interaction of the Octave and Trinity. All these become possible because of the paths forming the three columns and connecting every sefirah in a complex of circulation. Here is the original flow chart but so designed that a whole series of Worlds can function.

The origin of the paths has been subject to much speculation. Some put forward the concept that the Tree is in fact a geometric solid with the paths between the sefirot marking the mid-zone division of balanced function. Thus Hesed and Gevurah are separated but not parted. Others say that the sefirot were first formed, perhaps like crystals emerging out of a cosmic solution, and that the path patterns were the connecting rays of relationship. Yet others state that until two sefirot exist a path between them cannot be born, while another school says that as the Divine Lightning Flash unfolds down its zig-zag the subsidiary paths follow making the secondary links.

All of these concepts are each in their own way correct but perhaps the most significant fact for us is that some key has been lost. This explains why there are so many different interpretations of the paths by different schools down the ages. So here also is an area of study for our own time.

In order to demonstrate the state of understanding at this point a sample of views will be examined. What must be borne in mind is that the relationship between two sefirot not only includes the common element of both of them but the path's position on the Tree, its place in that particular triad or set of triads and which way the flow along it is moving. This, it will be remembered, is determined by the active and passive relationship of the sefirot. A complex analysis problem but one that becomes easier with time and familiarity in the way that diagnosis does to an experienced doctor.

The first thing we have to know about the paths is that there are

94

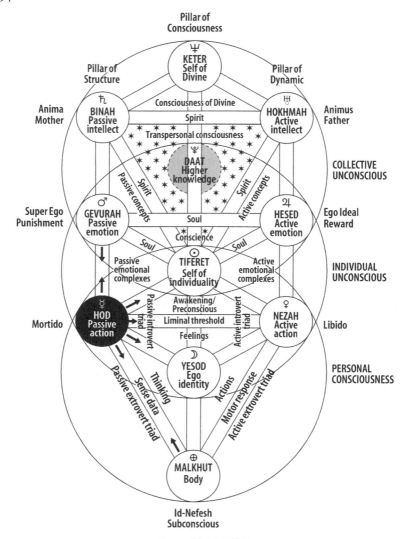

*Figure 28—PATHS*

*This is an example of how the paths work within the psyche. The sefirotic function of Hod is thought, black ink marks on a page, but translating them into words. Meanwhile, the arrow on the path to Gevurah is recognising a judgmental response as to whether what is said makes sense. Simultaneously, the arrows between Hod and Yesod stimulate an image within the ordinary mind that makes the Tree alive while the Self absorbs and files the experience, associated emotions and ideas throughout the mind, so influencing the whole psyche, both consciously and unconsciously. (Halevi).*

twenty-two of them. According to the most common system these are numbered, beginning after the tenth sefirah of Malkhut, and start at the top of the Tree with the Keter-Hokhmah path designated as number eleven. The sequence then follows the enumeration across to twelve in Keter-Binah, then thirteen down to Tiferet and so on, until we reach the thirty-second path of Yesod and Malkhut. This system is based on the three forces striking out from each sefirah as the Lightning Flash is unfolded with the triads closed as the Flash sequence hits the adjacent sefirah on its descent. It is a logical development, though not every Kabbalist would agree with it. It does show very clearly, however, a growth pattern, though it may be like an earthly lightning flash working from both directions simultaneously. Many people who use the Tree for personal development apply this particular system, identifying different paths by number and placing their own understanding of each connection between the sefirot. Such an example would be the path 31 between Hod and Malkhut which would be concerned with subjects relating to science and the study of the physical world, as against path 23, Hod-Gevurah, which would be perhaps an exercise in the development of critical discrimination about oneself. The significance of each path becomes more apparent as the Tree, particularly in relation to man, becomes known. Here we are only examining different ways of looking at the same phenomena.

It is said that the sefirot are objective and that the paths are subjective. In simple terms the sefirot always remain the same, like the position of the crown in England whose traditional cry is, on the death of a sovereign, 'The King is dead, long live the King.' This is no sentimental rite but the acknowledgement of a necessary constant which is above the fluctuations of time and governments. The sefirot are always the same in performing their function. If they were not, the relative Universe would collapse. A parallel analogue is seen in the constant elements forming a village society, anywhere and at any time. There are always the elders, the men and women, the adolescents and the children. Each person passes through different stages or initiations, be it in the jungle or on the city block corner, so that by maturity he has been the boy, the youth, the young married, the parent and so on. Almost everyone fills at some point one of these stations, either negatively or positively.

The paths are not constant in the same way as the sefirot. By nature they are subject to the two poles of the sefirot to which they are attached. They also carry negative, positive or neutral charges and

96

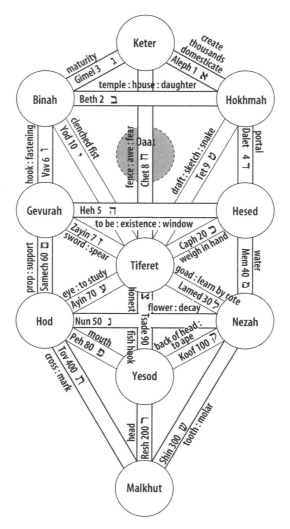

*Figure 29—LETTERS AND NUMBERS*
The idea that the Hebrew Aleph-Bet relates to the paths comes from the myth that
Existence is based upon Ten utterances of the Creator. Like Latin, Hebrew letters also
represent numbers. Out of this have come several systems. The reality is that the Tree
was initially numbered and lettered as a shorthand way of identifying a sefirah or
path quickly. Over the centuries, especially after the encounter with Greek philosophy
and science, new annotations were applied to the Bible, giving rise to Notaricon and
Gematria which were meant to reveal deeper aspects of the texts. However, such mind
games can mislead. This system, for example, makes words out of the root ideas
contained in each Hebrew letter. (Halevi).

take on the character required by the triads they participate in. They are like chameleons but with definite colours, only able to assume a certain range of variants. This is, as the word 'subjective' implies, because they are not the rulers of a situation.

Many attempts have been made to synthesise the ranges covered by each path and this next system may be the oldest. We can guess, as speculation allows, that the Hebrew language may have been re-formed while the Jews were captive in Babylon in the sixth century before the Common Era (BCE). This was possible because Hebrew was no longer a first language but would become so, it was hoped, when the exiles returned to Palestine. Much work was done, not unlike the efforts of the 19th and 20th century Zionists who brought Hebrew into the modern world with new words taken from other contemporary tongues. In Babylon it was a different problem. The solution they were seeking (whoever 'they' were who were behind this movement) was more than redesigning the Hebrew pictographs into Syriac letters. They were, it would appear, trying to restructure the actual root of the tongue so that it would act as a system within a system, as algebra does within the body of mathematics, but as applied to the five books of Moses, the Torah and the Tree of Life. From this sprang many later discoveries and, while some based on numerology were a very profound key to philosophy and the word structure of the Old Testament, many investigators became so enamoured with numbers and their meaning that they fooled themselves as well as many others. This is a phenomenon common to modern science as well, so perhaps one must accept these as failed experiments, along with the many unflying machines prior to the Wright brothers. However, these dead-end journeys into numerical fantasy do not detract from the genuine work done by the early rabbis who were making the most of a unique opportunity. The following is a glimpse into the research on their system being carried out at this present time. Like archaeology, only some of the foundations have been uncovered and while we can only guess at the magnificence of the palace that lies buried we only have a wing or a courtyard at most at this point to work on.

The Hebrew alphabet has more than sound values. It also has numerical designations, symbolic and cosmic meanings. The numerical values are simple and common to many ancient languages without a separate number system. Hebrew goes much deeper and has a whole metaphysic of allied numbers and families of words. This, however, is not our area of study and we must leave it to those who are familiar with the vast maze of meanings that may be extracted from such a versatile set of keys. If we look at the Tree we will see that besides the sequential numbering set out earlier, every path has a Hebrew letter assigned to it, twenty-two in all, of the alphabet. Each one of these has a numerical correspondence increasing in number towards Malkhut. This is again a study in its own right.

Of more intelligible interest to us are the root meanings or images formed by the letters. Up till about the eighth century of the Common Era (CE) Hebrew did not have written vowels so that many meanings could root back to a simple three-lettered word. The name Hod is a good example, as a glance through an English-Hebrew dictionary will show. It is from this common root word we get 'splendour' and 'to reverberate'. A little practical observation reveals that the title of this sefirah is no vague description but a very precise account of Hod's function on the elemental and action level of the Tree of Life.

Examining the letters and their root meanings, we begin to see another way of viewing the paths. Thus Aleph, in the Keter-Hokhmah path, means 'to create thousands', or 'to domesticate and civilise' while Beth according to another system of sequence on the Hokhmah-Binah path means 'a house, temple, daughter'. The Tree paths are developed further by this method which differs from the others in that it completes the triads as it goes along the Lightning Flash, instead of filling them in later. The images of the letters flow down the Tree, each symbol a key to a particular path. Ayin on the path between Hod and Tiferet means 'eye', or 'to study, to examine' which is appropriate to Hod looking at Tiferet, in the sense of the ordinary logical mind conferring with its essential nature; that is, the one representing Mercury, the god of information and communication addressing Apollo, the god of truth and illumination. This way of defining the different paths is very valuable and there is reason to believe, from current research, that a whole philosophy is to be dug out of the roots of the Tree and the ground beds of Hebrew. For instance, a way of reading the paths based on this system of lettering gives some interesting insights. The Nezah-Malkhut-Hod triad, and their perspective letters Shin, Nun, and Tov, form the root word of 'cycles, day, year and sleep' etc. The triad Hod-Nezah-Yesod forms, by their letters Nun, Koof, Peh, the root of the words 'to go round in a circle'. Hod-Nezah-Tiferet and their path letters form the root of 'lock in position, to be shod'. The letters of the Gevurah-Hesed-Tiferet triad form the word Zayin, Caph, Heh which is the root of 'purification', or 'cleanse' in all its senses. Binah, Hokhmah, and Tiferet and their letters Yod, Tet, Beth form the root of 'to make fertile, to improve'. The last triad, Keter-Hokhmah-Binah which give the letters Gimel, Beth, and Aleph, means 'reservoir of water', or 'underground system'. Incidentally, Adam derives from Keter, Hokhmah, and Hesed, the letters meaning 'blood', 'living', 'red' and 'man'. The letters of the Nezah-Malkhut-Hod triad form Seth the son of Adam—which also means 'the basis' or 'bottom'. Finally, the path letters from Hod-Gevurah, Gevurah-Binah, Binah-Keter, spell out Samech, Vav, Gimel which means to 'return to source', thus completing the whole cycle. While of advanced academic interest, these root words and letters give an insight into the detailed infrastructure of the Tree to be explored.

Yet another facet to the Hebrew alphabet are the planetary, zodiacal and elemental designations given in the ancient *Book of Formation*. In this early kabbalistic work the letters, when set out in the second sequence, also describe, according to the letter and its correspondence, the nature of the paths. Thus the path between Malkhut and Yesod, lettered Resh, is the path of Saturn which is a long hard rise, in human terms, through the material world. Here is an earthy intelligence, the patience-creating experience of seeing the Universe behind the outer surface of existence. This is a tough, gloomy path but one that develops strength and resilience. Here we have yet another key to the nature of the path, though the language of planets and zodiac may not be of our time. This creates many difficulties for those studying the Tree of Life for the residue of centuries of work, once so alive in its day, now only obscures the view. Ideas and symbols sometimes outlive their usefulness. If they are real archetypes they return in modified form, like the eternal Venus of each generation who reveals herself quite clearly despite changing fashion.

A third system which is related to the Tree and paths and is worth examining (even though it has been dimmed not so much by time as by superstition) is the Tarot pack. This is a collection of cards that first appeared in the Middle Ages. Today we only have the anaemic minor pack in the form of ordinary playing cards and several beautiful but probably incomplete versions of the major set.

Time, the remaking of new blocks, fashions and men adding their own ideas to the cards have, for the most part, left us only a fragmented image of what the pictures were like. As a system it is impressive with its graphic symbolism but there is something missing. However, we

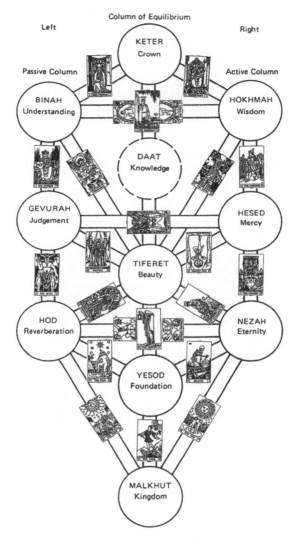

*Figure 30—TAROT*

The word Tarot can mean, in Hebrew, Teachings. *The origin of this pack of cards is unknown but there are clearly Hellenic and Egyptian as well as Jewish influences in its makeup. The ten cards in each of the four suits obviously relate to the sefirot and the four Worlds; while the twenty-two picture cards of the Major Arcana symbolise various levels, initiations and cosmic principles. One theory is that this shrewd model of a universal Teaching had to appear trivial because the Church condemned any threat to its dogma. Thus, if an occult group was burst in upon by the Inquisitors, they could say they were only playing cards.* (Tarot pack, 16th-19th century).

have reason to speculate that the Tree of Life is the frame of reference needed to complete it. Here are some possible clues.

The minor pack is composed of four suits, each made up of ten numbers beginning with the Ace. If we read the four suits as diagrams of the four Worlds or universes, we have a Diamond or Pentacle for Asiyyah, Hearts or Cups for Yezirah, Spades or Swords for Beriah and Clubs or Wands for the Azilutic world. Here we have Earth, Water, Air, and Fire again. Moreover, in the four royal cards attached to each suit we find the four levels contained within each World-suit Tree. Thus the Page of Wands is the Asiyyatic level in the Azilutic World and so on, while the Knight of Swords represents the Yeziratic level in the World of Creation. So it is with the Queen and King, both indicating the Beriatic and Azilutic levels in their respective suits. Kinship with the Kabbalistic Tree is indicated even more when we consider the suit of ten cards. Some schools see each number as corresponding to a sefirah, so that the Ace of Cups is the Keter of the Yeziratic World—indeed a Watery realm of changing forms—and the six of Wands as the Tiferet of the Azilutic realm. Others, looking further, maintain that the correspondence is even subtler as the sefirot are not so easily fixed. They say that each card represents a triad in that particular suit or World. Thus the six of Pentacles is the triad formed by Tiferet-Gevurah-Hesed of the Asiyyatic World while the ten of Wands is pivot to the triad Malkhut-Yesod-Hod in the Azilutic World. This is a complex matrix but gives a more definite picture of the Tree.

The major pack is made up of twenty-two picture cards. These are also specifically numbered and have Hebrew letters ascribed to them, though this may have happened before or after the Middle Ages. The imagery is very strange and evocative and anyone handling them can see how easy it would be for intentional or deliberate illusion to be introduced. Looking closely at the cards it is apparent that each is describing a condition or a set of laws at work, a principle or a direct statement. Whether they refer to the problem of lies, as defined by card fifteen—*The Devil* or black magician—or the subject of the laws of fate, as outlined in card ten or the *Wheel of Fortune*, we can never be sure because of the subjective nature of our own Hod minds. This exercise must be left alone until we have the key to follow this particular method—which to the over-imaginative and spiritually gullible only leads to intriguing, fascinating cul-de-sacs. Here we will look at them in terms of the Tree to illustrate how careful one must be when speculating with old material.

There are several systems whereby the twenty-two major Tarot cards may be placed on the paths of the Tree. While there may be a certain amount gained by such study, the very fact that independent and extremely intelligent versions have been set up on the paths makes the whole operation suspect. This does not invalidate the effects of the two illustrated examples, it merely shows just how subjective the paths are, therefore I advise the student of the Kabbalah to examine and learn from the Tree in its and his own terms and in words and images of his own time.

It is said that the Tarot pack was a philosophical machine that, when arranged in different ways, could answer all questions, be it about the nature of the world, man or God. We have now reached a point in our study where we can see that the Tree of Life is possibly a similar machine. Here we have a superb frame of reference, cosmic in its scale, divine in its reasoning. We may use it as men have done down the ages to look at our own times, see from the point of the eternal, the ephemeral world.

# 9. Practice

We have now completed our brief theoretical study of the Tree of Life. There is much more to be learned about its nature and mechanics but this can only be acquired through time and practice. The practical application of the Tree is most important for while we learn through Hod we must balance it with Nezah. In this way both columns of the Tree come into action, pivoted and observed from the central pillar.

The Tree of Life is a tool and a technique. It may be used in many ways, ranging from attaining full personal development to examining a relatively worldly body such as Parliament. From its scheme various psychological and physical disciplines can be planned. By obtaining understanding and mastery of the various aspects of the Tree extra power may be acquired and perceptions opened into new Worlds. These practices, however, require a skilled and reliable teacher who, though unusual in spiritual calibre, must be quite normal in his relation to the everyday world. A gifted but impractical instructor is not only useless but dangerous. One does not go mountain climbing with a guide who is even mildly unbalanced.

In a book such as this any attempt to show the Tree at work must be modest. Here we can only use the dim reflection of words to illustrate its potential. Therefore in this latter section we will look at various complete organisms and phenomena, to see how our cosmic microscope can throw light on to anything placed on the slide plate of Tiferet.

First we must set the rules for what can be examined. The prerequisite is that it is complete, that is, that it is an entire entity and not part of a unit. The heart is not such an object. It is big and important but only a nodal point in one of many cycles in the body. Nor is the body complete. At death the vital forces depart and the body ceases to function, quickly disintegrating back to its elements. Only a living man is complete. But we must remember that what we see walking down the street is just a thin momentary visible slice of his life. The rest exists, all his past and future ages and experiences are there present but out of sight, beyond Malkhut.

To examine any subject we must first define what it is, identify its essence. Thus with a man it is that which is peculiarly his and with him from the womb to the grave. Having seen this nucleus, we place it on the sefirah Tiferet. This is the main focus of our cosmic instrument. From this sharp image we can establish the other aspects in their respective sefirot. Having set the field of view, the relationships of the different parts of the whole become apparent. The Lightning Flash describes how the subject is formed, the central triads, the various inner levels and the side triads reveal the different interactional functions while the paths show in detail the interchange with the shifts of balance. This study will sometimes indicate a flaw and its remedy. The conclusions made from a session at the eye-piece of this extraordinary cosmic tool will often change the observer's view of the subject for ever for it is a curious fact that, having once seen quite mundane things in so deep and wide a glance, nothing ever appears as trivial as it did before.

We will begin the series of examinations with a look at the parliamentary system, because it is a quite easily recognisable human pattern. Accompanying each Tree will be a commentary, by no means full but enough to show a method of working. Later studies will be the examination of events and phenomena to show the application of the Tree in other ways. Finally, we will take again a look at man, aware that we are in ourselves a Tree, a perfect living instrument in our own right.

# *10. Exercise*

To anyone who has read so far and wishes to know more, it is important to realise the word Kabbalah means 'to receive'. However, there are four possible ways to understand the same communication. They are the mystical, the metaphysical, the allegorical and the literal. Here are the four Worlds and their keys. In order to practise unlocking doors I suggest as an initiation an exercise. This will perhaps place things in a personal context.

Find a quiet place, and sit comfortably with your spine
straight.
This is Malkhut.
Place your hands on your knees and close your eyes.
This is Hod.
Feel your pulse and breath.
This is Nezah.
Watch the images pass endlessly before your mind's eye.
This is Yesod.
Centre your attention away from the outer scene and the
inner pictures and sensations and focus on that part of you
that watches all this happening.
This is Tiferet.

Here is the lower face of Natural man. Above, on your own Tree of Life, is the upper face or the Supernatural man.

When you have become quiet and composed, the soul turned towards spirit, you may become one with yourself. Then you are indeed ready 'to receive'.

Practise this at least once a day.

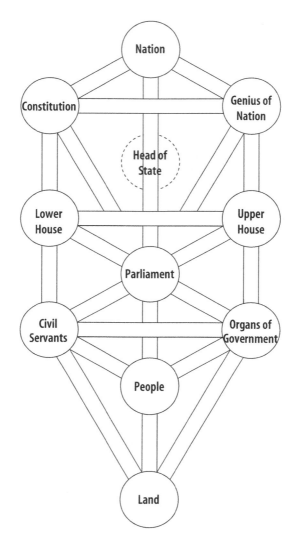

*Figure 31—GOVERNMENT*
*Here is the basic system by which democratic nations are governed. A nation is an area where a people shares the same general culture. This economic, political and social organism is monitored by various government agencies. At the centre is the seat of government with its two Houses to check each other's power. Above is the constitution or rules inspired by the genius of a people. At Daat is the Head of State who represents the spirit of the Nation. He or she gives authority to any law or government decision, such as peace or war. In theory the monarch or president should be above party politics. At the Crown is the destiny of the Nation. (Halevi).*

# 11. Parliament

The idea of a parliament is a very ancient one. Every primitive tribe, anywhere on the planet and in any age, has had its head man, its elders and laws designed for the common good of that community. Examining our modern parliamentary systems, providing they are not completely totalitarian—and even these have an underground Gevurah opposition—we see how the Tree of government functions, often unknowingly, in accord with cosmic principles.

Keter the Crown in this study may be several things. Besides its fountainhead position it can be the civilisation itself—of which a nation is a sub-culture—with its Christian or Buddhist ideal or even a physical Utopia of Communism. Both spiritual and material heavens indicate a direction, an upper realm for that nation. Keter may be Humanity itself, the Unity of all men to which the nation is joined in common bond. This could be confined to those at present living on the Earth or all the ancestors and descendants yet to come. Either way Keter is of vast import, the Creative emanations flowing down in generations to become manifest as a dynamic in Hokhmah.

In Hokhmah is the genius of a people. We see over long periods of history how national communities have distinct characteristics like a person. This people, for example, are inventors, that warriors, while those are religious by inclination. All nations contain everything human but one or several traits dominate its history, though from time to time these will ebb and flow in strength. The English, for instance, have a remarkable aptitude for invention and discovery. It is not without reason that the Industrial Revolution began in England, where the Malkhutian elements of coal and iron were exploited by this practical people. The Jews, for example, perhaps because of their long literacy, have certain intellectual skills whose abilities are not only used in the marketplace but in scholarship, medicine and government. A nation of wanderers they were, and are, often to be found as advisers but never leaders in their host country. The Scots, another scattered people, are intelligent, tough and serious with a particular talent for pioneering while their fellow Celts, the Irish, just as tough, are easy-going fighters and talkers.

The national image of a people, though often a distorted caricature, roots back to the spirit of the nation. This spirit is more powerful than is generally imagined. Not only does an Englishman become more English when he is abroad but one may recognise the power of his culture wherever the English have been, be it India or North America. King Arthur, Sir Francis Drake and Wellington embodied the spirit of England in their time. Churchill drew on this same spirit in 1940 and used its power to reinforce the British bulldog image. This may be regarded as old-fashioned thinking in the present time but bring any people under pressure and the Hokhmah of that nation will speak with a powerful voice.

The Binah on this Tree is the formulation of the tribe's character and needs into a set of mores or customs. In a sophisticated society this becomes the constitution. In the case of England, which has a thousand years of continuous development beginning with the installation of William the Conqueror (1066), the process has never been fixed while in comparatively recent times the American constitution was drafted at one historical point, though it is still being amended. Both these written and unwritten constitutions fulfil the same function. Situated at the head of the passive side of the Tree they make the powerful national energies conform. Without law there would be anarchy and the community as a whole would suffer. Therefore the Binah operation for the common good is vital.

This sefirah may, in a primitive tribe, be the crudest and most superstitious form of constraint but it will safeguard the tribe and guide it through internal and external difficulties, though it will be amended as the community progresses. Men will fight and die to defend Binah, though they know nothing of its purpose beyond a general principle. The English Magna Carta, though of no particular benefit to commoners, has been held up by the Englishman as a symbol of his rights for seven centuries. In it he recognises the written declaration of his protection under the law. Here is the constraining yet beneficial quality of Binah, for while it creates duties it grants privileges; thus we get a phrase in the American Declaration of Independence: 'We hold these truths to be self evident, that all men are created equal.' Here is the American dream—and nightmare. This is the scale of Binah. Placed opposite to Hokhmah it is concerned with great principles, not petty rules.

Following the Lightning Flash we cross to the invisible sefirah of Daat. This position is occupied by the Head of State who is, theoretically, above the ordinary law. In England the sovereign holds the position of constitutional monarch, rather like a crowned president. The Monarchy is on the main axis of the Tree. It has vertical and direct connection with the Parliament and thereby the people. As ruler, the monarch held the land or Malkhut, given by God, signified by Keter. The people were at Yesod while Parliament was at Tiferet. The monarch claimed the divine right to rule. Charles I believed that he could do as he pleased without the consent of the House of Commons. This led to the English Civil War and the establishment of the Commons' supremacy.

In England a bill only becomes law on the sovereign's assent, the Crown's theoretically direct contact with Keter relating it to Divine Will. That is why governments may fall in Britain but Parliament continues. The Crown, embodied in this or that sovereign was, as in ancient China and Japan, connected with heaven. This gave the royal prerogative of mercy and many other privileges traditionally granted to heads of state. The pale residue is still present at coronations, inaugurations and state occasions. Anyone who witnessed the funeral of President Kennedy was seeing more than the burial of an Irish immigrant's great-grandson.

Daat is the mystique of royalty, the curious aura surrounding a president. The people no longer see the human being but sense the presence of something closer to the divine than themselves. The President and the Queen fill a position which possesses magic. Anyone who dons the robe of head of state has to appear, if not be, perfect. The invisible becomes visible in the embodiment of that person. As individuals they vanish, in the way that a spiritually developing man who reaches this point in himself disappears into Keter. This is the quality of Daat.

Hesed is seen in the Upper House of any parliament. In England it is the Lords, in the United States the Senate. Most democratic countries now have two Chambers, one to check the other before a bill becomes law. The Upper Chamber, theoretically, represents the elders of the tribe who make sure that the Lower Chamber is working in the community's interest. With their position on the Tree they have access to Hokhmah, the spirit of the nation, and while they do not draft the laws they are expected to refer to the genius of their country as a check and modify unjust or expedient legislation. Often composed of

110

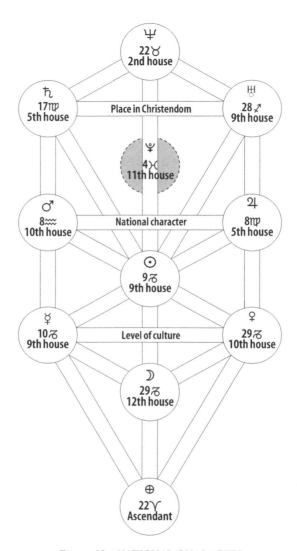

*Figure 32 — NATIONAL CHARACTER*
*Nations, like people, are born, mature and die. They also have birth charts that define their character and fate. Here is the horoscope of England. This entity was born at twelve noon on Christmas Day, 1066 when William the Conqueror was crowned in London. England has a Capricorn Sun, Pisces Moon and Aries Ascendant. The rest of the planets are set out according to their Sign and House. The combination indicates that the English are essentially a stable, conservative but enterprising people whose Watery and seemingly wimpish persona conceals a strategic, manipulative and occasionally violent disposition. (Halevi).*

older men who are usually past the zenith of their political ambition, their view is less biased and more generous. In England this is the highest court in the land, though still beneath the authority of the Throne. Here are men and women gathered from a wide range in life. Originally the Lords Spiritual and Temporal, their ranks now include trade unionists, judges, industrial magnates and even actors and writers. Here in England, which is perhaps the most politically mature country in the world, archbishops argue moral points with journalists on an equal footing, both aware that in the House of Lords they are the long-view guardians of the unwritten British constitution. The quality of the Upper Chamber is greatness and all the attributes of Hesed. Even in the former Soviet Union this sefirah was recognised, as the people sensed instinctively that there must be a higher court even in a one-party State.

The lower chamber in the British system is the House of Commons. This demonstrates very clearly the nature of Gevurah. It is a place of contention—how else could it be with a two or more party system? The British actually pay an MP to be the leader of the opposition. His job is to test the government's policy, seek every chink in its armour, hack off bad pieces of a bill, smash anything the opposition considers unjust while the party in power has to defend its proposals. This is the sefirah of Mars. Here is the ordinary outer emotion of a man. This is the Aye and Nay, the mundane judgements, the assessments, the point of decision with each clause argued out across the floor of the chamber. There is even a semi-military protocol in most Parliaments, rules of debate, so that the verbal conflict does not become a physical riot. Bitter exchanges are reported in the press as a government wins or is defeated. The atmosphere occasionally gets extremely emotional and in some more volatile countries tables and chairs fly across the chamber. In Britain they actually have a Serjeant-at-Arms who escorts any miscreant, be he an MP or a member of the public, from the chamber. This is Gevurah but in control, that is, beneath the direct influence of Binah above. Under rule the Lower House works well, always referring to the constitution and checked by the Upper House opposite in Hesed. It is here the laws are hammered out in detail, be it in the chamber proper or in committee. However, while the Commons or Congressmen may determine which way a policy will go, it is still finally subject to the rest of the Tree.

Tiferet is Parliament. It is all the pomp and pageantry, the authority and the power of the country seen in its parliamentary building set in the middle of the capital city. Here is the central focus of political power for the rulership of the state. Usually impressive in architecture, it must be seen to function. Beside the everyday customs that reveal its authority, such as the House of Commons not being able to begin its business till the Mace, the symbol of parliament, is in its place, so the Sovereign must open each session. The Queen's ride in a coach, surrounded by the horsemen of the Life Guards, is not a parade for tourists. Her short journey from Buckingham Palace to Westminster is part of the Tiferet activity of Beauty. Situated on the middle column at the point of many intersections, the opening of Parliament finds the building jammed with Lords and MPs, distinguished visitors and many other people privileged to be there. These occasions bring all the Tree of the government of Britain together with the Sovereign seated on the throne representing the presence of the continual line of history as manifest at that moment. Tiferet is, in the Lightning Flash or Octave, the Thing itself. Under our cosmic microscope it is Parliament, an object which is not just the Palace of Westminster or the people in it. Nor is it the quaint customs or uniforms; neither is it the statute book nor the political parties. It is all these things, both particular and general. Its quality runs through the meaning of government, so that it shines like the Sun—bright or dim over a whole country, bringing detriment or benefit according to the intelligence of its electorate.

Nezah is all the organs of government. In Britain these are the departments and ministries, also the services and all those organisations concerned with running the country. Generally, as in the case of the tax collectors, their function is cyclic, often coinciding with the seasons. The Department of Trade and Industry and the Department for Environment, Food and Rural Affairs are good examples. Some departments may be concerned with the Police while others administer Education and collect taxes. Yet others run the country's transport system while another Ministry will take care of the environment and pollution. All these are Nezah activities, the involuntary process required to keep a living body, or the economy, healthy. This includes the defence services who, like white blood corpuscles, are designed to protect the national organism from invasion. Any country that allows its defences to weaken, unless it has a powerful ally, soon dissolves and is absorbed by another. History is full of such stories: the Roman Empire eventually collapsed because of internal corruption—or disease. The vitality of a country is contingent on its wealth and

*Figure 33—PARLIAMENT*
*This form of government began in medieval England, in which the feudal system of*
*King, Lords and Commons met at Westminster to talk about national issues. The*
*commoners, who generated the wealth of the kingdom, exerted real power and*
*eventually executed a king who believed he had a Divine right to overrule Parliament.*
*The objection to an overbearing Crown precipitated the American Revolution. Here*
*Englishmen fought over the rights of Englishmen. Ironically, in the American system*
*the President has more power than the British monarch. (Palace of Westminster,*
Doré, 19th century).

vigour, that is on an economic sub-Tree of Life which supplies the bounty of resource. The power in wealth and people gives the Foreign Office or State Department its authority and military weight in the world outside. No one listens to a poor country's cause, however just.

Nezah is the machinery of government, the interdepartmental machinations. The Benefits Agency pays out, whatever party is in government. The Post Office, except when it is on strike, keeps—like the state radio—the nervous system of the nation going. The daily delivery of electricity and gas bills, licences and a dozen other public demands are just links in a national Nezahian chain of cycles vital to the country's wellbeing.

Hod in the Tree of government is its civil service. These are the mercurial data-gatherers, the myriads of forms sent out and returned to collect a vast amount of information varying from your income to a full census on the whole community. The material netted by this constant casting is stored, at least for a year, until it is out of date. Here are the great banks of files on social security, health, legal and financial matters. With the government computer, the Hod element is complete.

Other Hod activities are the official communications. This can range from leaflets to instruct on how to claim a tax rebate to simple political propaganda. The publicity campaign on the decimalisation of the British pound is a good example.

Special departments designed to deal with specific problems come under Hod. These may advise companies concerning trade abroad, or give information about new towns planned or areas to be opened up. Advisory bureaux at all levels of administration come into this sefirah, as do index systems, and the access to facts only a large concern like a government can afford to investigate. These would be sections that look at new inventions, like the Defence Research Agency or NASA, and many other investigatory bodies. Many of these would be linked with the universities which, of course, also fit into the Hod activity of the country.

Obvious functions such as the country's telecommunications relate to this sefirah and so do the links with the outside world, including the secret services like the CIA. Here are the customs and excise, the immigration sections, as well as the government-sponsored trading missions and trade fairs. Her Majesty's Stationery Office is pure Hod, as is any government White Paper. Every letter bearing the cypher 'On Her Majesty's Service' belongs to this activity, as does the despatch box sent to the Queen containing documents for her attention. For as said, until the royal signature is signed and sealed, a bill cannot become law but remains Hod.

Civil servants often draft bills well ahead of their times. This is because with their analyses of information they can anticipate what a minister may want. These are frequently worked out in detail, only to be modified on the floor of the House of Commons. Here is Hod in service beneath Gevurah, although its loyalty is primarily towards the incorruptible parliamentary ideal of Tiferet.

Yesod is the people, relating to the Moon. However, they change from time to time, sometimes reflecting, sometimes reacting to circumstance, be it parochial or international. The people on this scale are similar to the sea, their tidal mood putting that government in and throwing that one out of the parliament house, leaving it perhaps high and dry halfway through what it thought was to be the second leg of a good term of office.

Yesod is the realm of dreams and mirages and the politician knows that his public image will make or mar his career, with every TV interview and speech on the hustings affecting his chances to become a Prime Minister or President. An aspiring candidate takes great care to build up a good Yesodic picture of himself, slanting it to show he is aware of the man in the street and his problems; though once in power, his eye is on different matters. All the political campaigners over the world know that there has to be excitement in order to move the masses even to vote, unless they are forced to exercise their right by law. Bands, meetings, even a little heckling and fighting, will at least generate some wave motion in the population. The people on the whole are passive, living their daily round much the same, only occasionally stirred by a major condition such as war or depression. For the most part they read the papers, watch TV, hear the news on car radios unmoved, except when it personally involves them, and when some catastrophe occurs elsewhere it soon passes from the Yesodic screen of the nation, fading into the ever-changing cycle of work, play and sleep. The people are the power of the nation. Their endless generation supplies the energy to work the natural wealth. From this point come the men and women who, for whatever motivation, climb up the Tree of Parliament. It is this sefirah that supports parliament, yet must be governed by it so that it does not fall into anarchy. The laws are made to contain but protect the people, so that the meanest individual has justice even though it may be he versus the Crown in the lowest or highest court in the land.

Malkhut is the land. It is the earth itself, the rivers, lakes and the surrounding seas. It is the air above and the right to the sky. Before men came, England was an island wilderness. Here the natural laws of the jungle were at work. On man's arrival the balance changed, the forests and marshes were cleared and the mineral wealth of the land exploited. Whether this is good or bad is not for us to judge for we must see man's contribution from a planetary level to see the whole. All that can be said is that man is the spearhead of evolution and his pushing back of the wilderness part of a cosmic design—pollution, when corrected, included. Our Parliamentary Tree is literally rooted in the soil. People cannot live without space, be it a farm or a small flat. Here we see how in Britain the Crown holds the land, a gift from God, for the people. Over the years this has appeared to have become a mere symbol. But in fact we see, with the evolution of social conscience, that both capitalist and communist societies recognise that the duty of the Parliament is not to the political or wealth-oriented aristocracy but to the people as a whole. Here once again the inherent Tree of a complete organism asserts itself. If it does not—and we witness again and again throughout history the results when governments do not allow the natural flow of the Tree—revolution breaks out and there is an attempt to set up a balanced order again. In violent storms the Tree of Life shakes, like any other, disturbing its equilibrium. For example, sometimes the people rise up and mob rule, like the Yesodic nightmare of the Reign of Terror in Paris, takes over the government. Occasionally a man in the position of head of state actually begins to believe he is God rather than His steward over a nation. More than one dictator has fallen on this one. In most cases of crisis one side of the Parliamentary Tree is over-emphasised. An example of this was pre-Civil War England resulting in Cromwell's Commonwealth which was also unbalanced, but in its Puritanism.

Here then, as our first exercise, is the Parliamentary Tree of Life. The same technique may be applied to a commercial company or a university or any complete organisation.

# 12. God and Mammon

In this exercise we take two Trees simultaneously in order to study parallel principles. Here we also follow how the Tree develops and establishes itself at each level. Taking the two poles of celestial and terrestrial wealth we set up a contrast, showing how even Mammon has to obey cosmic law.

Beginning with the financial Tree, we take Hokhmah as the first manifestation. Here is born the concept of a token of exchange. This is a global idea common to all but the most primitive communities. The notion of money is a powerful abstraction, requiring an appreciation of a level well above exchange and barter. This is the creation of a symbol, be it metal, shell, stone or paper, which makes possible a complete flexibility of transaction. By the mutual acceptance of currency many new things are possible for a tribal economy. A large community with different peoples exchanging multifarious goods and skills can grow larger still. Men may pay for services they themselves cannot perform with currency earned by their own particular talents. Without money, that vital, neutral but commonly valued token, modern civilisation could not have evolved. Money is one of the three forces in the economic triad of activity. Principally the intermediary, it may also be the activator or the result. Whichever way, the first tribesmen who saw that a form of money was the solution to the exchange of goods and services problem opened up a vast new field that was to affect mankind greatly. This glimpse of a principle perhaps came from a profound insight into the cosmic law of work and payment which runs throughout Creation.

Taking the same sefirah but on the Tree of Philosophy, Hokhmah would be the enlightenment of a Teacher. Here the flash of illumination coming down from Keter reveals the intention of the Divine. The Teacher may have received this insight in one brilliant vision or a succession of such moments over a lifetime. Aware at the level of Wisdom or inner intellect, he perceives the Will of the Creator in everything and sees the Universe and men permeated through with

*Figure 34—MONEY*

*This Roman coin and every modern bank note is a convenient illusion. They are, in themselves, almost valueless and yet people will work hard, scheme and even kill to acquire more. Currency is a kind of catalyst that allows trade to proceed. But there is yet more to this stamped metal disc. The head of a Caesar speaks of political power. Millions of people could use it in Western Europe, North Africa and the Middle East when they were under Rome rule. However, the illusion can become a delusion when the financial markets are unbalanced. This can occur when confidence fails. This happened in 1929 when there was a major negative planetary configuration. Then people responded to a global mood of uncertainty which resulted in the Wall Street crash as stock markets and shares became worthless. (Roman coin).*

emanations. To humanity the Teacher appears to be the fountainhead, the human radiance through which flows the glory of God. The Master, situated at the position of Hokhmah, sends out through the three succeeding paths the driving force of a profound philosophy or world religion. Men look to him as the representative of God on Earth or the exponent of divine wisdom. He is the ideal, the Prophet, the Buddha, the Messiah, the source of the inspiration.

The tradition based on his teaching is formulated in Binah. Here, with understanding, the sayings of the Master are ordered into precepts. St Paul spent his life doing this for Christ. Based on the Teacher's life, a whole set of outlooks is evolved. The Master's view of the Universe is rationalised and his position in the cosmic hierarchy fixed, even if there is no obvious ladder of evolution. It is at this point that the various eightfold paths, thirteen principles of faith and ten commandments are laid down. It is here that the organisation of the religion begins and the rituals, customs and practices of that tradition are worked out, though perhaps over hundreds of years. Binah, being the passive mother sefirah, imbues the tradition with all the conservative, submissive qualities common to each religion or philosophy. Nothing must be changed. Occasionally, when the form pillar is too active, orthodoxy becomes sometimes as powerful as the Master's word, sometimes more so, so that men trying to relive the original Master's way are destroyed by his Church. This happens when the letter of the Law becomes more important than the Spirit; in kabbalistic terms when the passive Binah becomes active. This usually occurs long after the Master has taken his physical departure and his followers, fearing to lose contact, preserve the outward form rather than the essence of his teaching.

In the Tree of Economics, Binah is the formulation of the principles of finance. Here, well respected rules must be set up so that transactions on a scale larger than the village market place are possible. A high level of trust must be created and facilities for lending and borrowing (to offset time lag between outlay and profit) be made available. This requires organisation; the setting up of a banking system with its numerous checking points and receiving and distribution centres. Good reliable communications are vital and the type of men involved in running such a system must have unimpeachable reputations. The different levels of commerce, ranging from local to national, have to be identified, also the recognition of various kinds of activity on the economic ladder. A whole picture of the state of industry, the stability

of a community, has to be assessed so that calculated risks with a view
to profit and economic development can be sponsored. The effect of
this system has to be taken into account for by nature it must be
conservative to maintain its reliability, yet speculative enough to
expand. Banking traditions grow and the men running the institutions
are expected to conform to the financial house's image. No national
or international banking concern can afford big mistakes; besides,
there are the mutual obligations to other banking organisations, all of
which form a global financial system.

In financial terms Hesed represents wealth, be it in hard currency,
gold, oil, goods or national skills. Britain, for example, is a trading as
well as a manufacturing nation. Her wealth is not just the gold stored
in the Bank of England. She certainly produces much industrial
material but she also sells her know-how and many unseen services in
insurance and overseas investment. These resources, visible and invisible,
are her wealth and the value of the pound sterling is backed up by the
health of her economy. This is Hesed and it must expand in order to
continue the Lightning Flash down the Tree of Britain's prosperity.
Should a slump set in and Britain not be able to fill the Hesed sefirah
actively, a depression will follow as the flow down the rest of the Tree
diminishes. A quick glance at the paths will show where it will hit.
Hesed, for obvious reasons, must always be expansive and here we
observe the larger Tree of world trade. With the financial news always
speaking of increasing gross national product we clearly sense the
impulse of a vast global network of economies, each Hesed in each
country contributing to the world's wealth, be it a natural resource, for
instance of oil, or the highly technical skill of the aero-industry.

In Hesedic terms on the spiritual Tree, this sefirah means the quality
of being or the spiritual vitality present in a religion or philosophy.
This may take the form of an expanding body of evolving people;
saints, thinkers and men of action, of that Way. Such a phenomenon
is seen in the *Zohar* period of the Kabbalah, in the Church and
Scholasticism at the time of Thomas Aquinas and in Islam during the
great era of the Mevlevi Dervishes. Movements such as these are
powerful in their influence, in that they reinforce the energy side of
the Tree to balance with the doctrine aspect of the form column. These
Hesedic activities are also important because they contain the expanding
impulse of the original teaching which is not only carried on over time
but is spread out from its place of origin. Any religion or philosophy
that does not move or grow, dies; usually because of the constraint of

an over-active Binah which creates a conservative Establishment which insists on preserving a teaching as a dogma. This inevitably discourages the Hesedic principle of taking in new and genuine converts, an absolutely necessary process if a Tradition is to survive. History is littered with dead and dying esoteric movements whose leaders did not realise that the growth point of their Tradition was not at the formal centre of their elect company but occurred more often in unscheduled meetings which flower when directly prompted by Hesed. Such graced gatherings, often unknown to the official hierarchy, are connected, at that moment in time, to the inner circle of that Tradition. As so often happens, this phenomenon is disagreeable to the Establishment who believe only they possess the Truth. The history of the Church bears witness in its initial rejection of many of its visionaries, like Teilhard de Chardin and St Teresa, and Orthodox Judaism had the same problem with Baal Shem Tov and Spinoza. Conventional Islam had actually to destroy Al Hallaj. Hesed is the dynamic of a spiritual Tradition. Standing below Wisdom and receiving from Understanding and Knowledge, Hesed feeds down into Nezah and Tiferet and across to Gevurah. Hesed is the deep emotional reservoir of a Tradition, the powerhouse vital to its longevity and growth.

Gevurah, in spiritual terms, is discipline. This is the focusing of the Hesed expansion. Without discipline the energy generated in Hesed would be lost. This application of the martial aspect of the sefirah is very marked in the monastic tradition with its strict rule and obedience, the latter directly related to the effect of Binah, the great Mother Church above. Discipline means to follow, though often an overactive interpretation is seen as a method of making the followers conform. While it is absolutely necessary for the love and power coming from Hesed to be controlled (or one has what is known as a stupid saint) this confining and channelling of religious emotion must not be fanatical. In extreme terms, when Gevurah is the master and not the servant, we have both the zealot and puritan operating under the jurisdiction of Binah's authority. Here is the Spanish Inquisition. The correct balance lies in the discipline being not for its own sake but for the Tree as a whole.

In schools of philosophy, Gevurah is not only the rule of conduct but also the discipline of intellect. Here is good argument, intelligent discussion and discrimination. Inspired visions are fine but they must be sharply focused or the meaning is diffused and lost. The power of discernment belongs here and is easily recognised in the Platonic

*Figure 35—REVELATION*
*Most religions are founded upon the vision of a prophet. The experience is usually the*
*result of a moment of Grace, a deep meditation or a long contemplation of God, the*
*universe and the human situation. Their followers then formulate their master's*
*teaching into a mode that is accessible to the masses. Here is the division between the*
*esoteric and an exoteric. The former is called the 'House of Israel' or elder souls and*
*the latter the 'Children of Israel'. Over time, animal people displace the original*
*school of the soul and create an 'Orthodox' organisation which is designed to*
*imprison people, the exact opposite of the aim of the Master's revelation. (Bank's*
*Bible, 19th century).*

dialogues. This is insight, well controlled and lucid in articulation with a razor-edged sense of true and false placed in the service of the highest cause.

In finance Gevurah is the level of practical banking. It is here that the day-to-day adjustments are made; in the West, on Wall Street, the London Stock Exchange and the Bourse in Paris. In each of these cities the banks perform (with their computer watchers on the various indices) the fine balance of a house of cards. These cards are the delicate relationships of trust, the myriad transactions dealing in millions that flow back and forth. Here one industry blooms, there one fades. The price of steel rises, that of grain sinks. The Dollar is steady, the Pound rises while the Euro may be devalued and the Yen revalued. Every moment is full of new possibilities. A country containing a huge reservoir of oil may have a revolution threatening the flow of energy and wealth from that area. Fast adjustments have to be made, quick decisions to switch to a stable area. The price rises. Capital, private or government, is released or held in check to maintain the market. Perhaps the price of gold, because of a political crisis, rises; so this financially barometric metal is shifted from one vault to another. The buying and selling is fast and furious. In a falling market the atmosphere is frenetic, only a tight discipline and network of trusts holds a dangerous situation together. Even governments can be frightened by a series of bad decisions and panic selling. Only the over-riding governor of the country's treasury, the Bank of England for Britain, can check a bad run by altering the bank rate. This is Gevurah at work in economics. Here is clean-cut decisiveness, based on hard facts and the mood of a market. It takes a military type of temperament to size up the day-to-day situation and take action that might well have to be reversed tomorrow. The apparent poker-face disposition of the financier is absolutely necessary. The best soldiers are the ones who never lose their cool.

Tiferet on the financial Tree is the particular monetary system of that area or country. Thus we have the pound sterling area centred on London, to which are linked several countries not all in the British Commonwealth. Its face value is the pound and what is seen on each bank note is the Queen of Britain's face. Here is the symbol of stability, tradition, a whole history of reliability stretching over what was the British Empire. The expression 'safe as the Bank of England' was no idle boast. It literally meant anyone carrying British currency, during Britain's primacy, could change it into the local money anywhere in the civilised world. This was because of the back-up of Britain's industrial and military might. Here was an imperial economy, capitalist in outlook (the flag and trade went together), powerful and profitable. Most of the Empire's wars were fought over trade. The Anglo-French confrontation in the eighteenth century over India and North America is a prime example. On the other hand Tiferet can be a communist economy. Here the party, theoretically representing the people, takes charge of the finance of the country. Industry is nationalised and so is banking but the same economic laws apply at Binah, though the profit goes to the state rather than to the private investor. In Russia the image of the currency is much the same. The rouble rates just as much interest in the lives of Russians as the dollar does to Americans.

Tiferet, in religion or philosophy, is the face by which it is known in the world. Into Tiferet flow the paths of the Teacher, the tradition, the driving power and the discipline, not to mention the direct flow through Daat from the Crown of Keter. Here is the focus of a belief, as seen in the ritual. Be it the Mass, the reading of the Law, meditation or the whirling of the Dervishes, all express that tradition. Vast buildings bear witness to the body of each particular sect, their walls, roofs and floors speaking in stone of their theology while the rites proclaim their persuasion. The Great Temple in Jerusalem, St Peter's in Rome, the Kaaba Shrine at Mecca, are more than mere physical settings for their religions. The concept of the Temple drew the Jews back to Palestine after two millennia of exile.

From the viewpoint of philosophy a set of writings like the kabbalistic *Zohar* acts as the Tiferet. The Tree of Life itself is a symbol as well as a working diagram. The writings of Plato have attracted thinkers down the ages, some of whom may never have read a word of his but practise the platonic approach. The Islamic Sufis have a collection of stories around which a whole teaching is focused. None of these works are the thing itself yet people can relate to the teaching through them.

The invisible sefirah Daat, in the philosophical and religious context, might be likened to the spirit above such a movement. It is here that the Divine emanation comes directly into focus. Perhaps this occurs during the Catholic Mass, during the Cohen's blessing of the people in the Jewish high festivals or during the ecstasy of the Dervish turning—no one but the recipients can tell. This is indeed the point of transformation when the Objective World enters the relative Universe.

In the realm of commerce Daat is knowledge. While the saint or philosopher may come to know about the sublime, the financial genius knows in his field about economics. Such a man though of mundane outlook might be a merchant banker or even a prime minister, like Benjamin Disraeli who bought the vital shares in the Suez Canal company. It required a flash of vision to see the waterway as an important link in Britain's Far East trade and a master's touch to move secretly and quickly, overriding more conventional buyers. This action proved a stroke of genius for Britain who would have been, at the height of her Empire, at the mercy of whoever held the canal. Another seer at this level was the medieval Portuguese Prince, Henry the Navigator. He foresaw not just the new shipping lanes to be opened up but the vast influx of Oriental and African wealth flowing in.

Daat is an invisible sefirah—it is not consciously reachable unless certain prerequisites have been fulfilled on the economic Tree. That is why financial crises are common throughout the world. No government can ever be really objective, so we get a continuous shift from one sefirah to another on either side of the two outer pillars.

In economic practice Nezah is the circulation of wealth. It is also industry. It is here that raw materials are converted into goods or effort into services. This is the most obvious part of the economic Tree. In every country the factories and their plants compose the vast muscles of industry, using up huge amounts of fuel. Here is the cycle of production, the endless chain of product and consumer. This is the autonomic system of a country slowly processing metals, minerals, natural materials and recycled trash into the national products that are to be used locally or exported. Into this cycle flow imports, some in a crude state, others already refined. This flow includes sophisticated materials, tools, luxuries, all facilitated by the free interchange of money. A five-pound note may never leave the bank vault but during a day's transaction it may have been lent to buy a boat of grain, then repaid in part of a debt on some nickel which is as yet still in the ground. The same note might change hands several hundred times in its roughly six-month life round the pockets, purses and tills of a country. This is the same as the blood system in a man, the coins as corpuscles, in a constantly circulating chain of wages and prices.

Nezah in philosophy or religion is practice. A man may be a Jew or a Christian by birth but it may merely be nominal. The practising Moslem performs his daily obligations as part of his life. The devout Jew binds on his phylacteries without question and no person professing

126

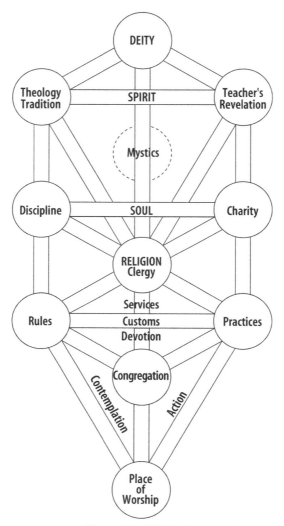

*Figure 36—RELIGION*

*Here the Tree reveals the various levels within a tradition. At the bottom is the appropriate Temple and its congregation. In the lower triads are the three initial Ways to approach the Deity. These are governed by local customs and practices which are implemented in daily, weekly and monthly services. The clergy of any particular sect, if it is not corrupt, will be disciplined and open-minded, taking care of their own souls as well as others'. Above, although not always recognised, are the mystics who keep the tradition alive while theologians build upon the Teacher's original revelation, either to clarify the Teaching, at best, or make more obscure, at worst. Even Kabbalah has suffered from the accretion of misinterpretation.* (Halevi).

to be a practising Christian would omit his prayers. There are of course degrees in all this. A man may merely pass through all the motions of religious practice. This was the problem of the Pharisees; to be seen to perform is not the same as actively performing and a devotee must refer to Hesed, the active sefirah above, for real concurrence. Certainly a man may belong to a religion (his Tiferet) but this may be through pride of race or tradition. This is not a real qualification. He must practise his religion as an integral part of his daily cycle, like eating and sleeping and all the processes of Nezah, before he is a really committed believer. For the philosopher, he too must practise. He must test everything he sees. To observe is not enough. He has to relate his life constantly to what he knows. There is no place for intellectual schizophrenia. He must act according to the principles to which he subscribes. If he follows the Greeks he must be able to analyse. If he is a Sufi he must keep breaking habits. As a Jew he will constantly refer everything to the Torah or the Tree. As one of the chief Jewish prayers says: 'no matter whether he is lying down or standing up, walking or eating'. This is the application of Nezah.

Hod is the theory of philosophy. It is also the reams of verbiage written down over the centuries on matters of religion. The Middle Ages, up to the seventeenth century, produced great numbers of books on theology and even wars were fought over matters of doctrine. This is the passive form pillar playing an active role with Gevurah and Binah backing up Hod's theological precedents. In philosophy, Hod is the sefirah where the subject is talked about. As the word 'about' suggests, it never actually deals with the experience but comments on it. Nezah teaches it, the inner realm responds but Hod, while knowing of it, can only (like this book) describe it in second—or third-hand—terms. On the positive side Hod enables the man to be introduced to powerful ideas. With its outward-pointing orientation it can identify, taste and smell the echo of reality, though it always thinks that it has direct contact with the outside world. The ordinary logical mind and its memory bank is useful but not an authority on such subjects as philosophy and religion. It knows the line, verse and chapter but not the meaning of the content, though it may claim it. It will, however, remind you of the volume containing the right quotation or prompt you to meditate at the regular time. It will even inform you that something deep occurred inside your being, though it will not know what it is, however much it will try—and try it will.

Hod is trade on the economic Tree. As the mercurial ordinary mind and senses act as the go-between in the inner and outer world, so Hod is the process of transaction in commerce. On the Bank of England five-pound note it says 'I promise to pay the bearer'. This is a word bond, no more than a printed offer which everyone trusts. Every day, over shop counters and a myriad other places where money changes hands, this promise is honoured. So much so that even criminals trust it enough to want to steal large quantities of these bits of paper, a true mercurial action.

Hod is the point of communal interaction, the grass roots of economics. A great industry may be founded by millions in capital but it is maintained by Everyman paying his electric bill, buying a car or even going to the movies. The whole industrial effort is directed at everyman. The vast numbers of consumers lose sight of the fact that each one has in his or her purse the means to finance not only the whole of industry but the wealth and standing of a country. A nation may be large but, unless trade is fast and high, it cannot afford the basics of life. These are financed from wages and taxes, every cent and penny adding to an immense river of money flowing throughout the system. The debit card sidesteps the coin and note but it is still Hod. The blank cheque is invalid until signed. With all the attributes of Mercury the whole basis of money at this level is verbal promise. This is the only way the financial system can work for a producer, like a car worker, cannot use a spare wheel for his pay, nor can a servicer, like an insurance broker, eat his own policies, however vital to life he claims them to be.

Yesod on the financial Tree is the mass of the people and their standard of physical living. It is each person's personal wealth and how much he can earn in that particular economic system. He is not only the producer but the buyer of the produce of that Tree and receives, by the various paths, the benefits of its industry and organisation. He can also receive its discrepancies so that, should a recession occur, he suffers the imbalance of each sefirah. The pound or dollar in his pocket is the Tiferet of his economic Tree and he sits directly underneath its aegis. It is also to be seen that Yesod forms part of a Hod and Nezah triad which describes the cycle of manufacturing, selling and buying, of which he is a vital link. The great financial crash of 1929 occurred partly because the masses could not afford to buy the goods they were making. If trouble, for instance civil disturbance, occurs in a community, this affects production and trade and therefore the people themselves. If the stimulus disturbing the people is strong enough, like the injustice of land distribution, a revolution will be incurred that will bring about a change in the whole of the economic system. Yesod is the people and their ideal of values.

In spiritual matters, Yesod indicates the individual's level. A mass is composed of individuals but, unlike economics, each man is more than a mere unit of production and consumption. He contains the whole Tree within himself. At Yesod he will reflect outwardly the face of a Jew or Moslem. Inwardly he may be in fact a great or gross man. This is his choice. He may choose merely to imitate his father or even a master, acting as a reflection of his words and actions. The way his teacher smokes a cigarette can sometimes make a greater impression than what he is saying. His method of questioning may be copied without any understanding. Here is the persona, the bridge to learn, the barrier to imprison. The honest man who does not fulfil all the obligatory devotions may possess more wisdom than the keeper of the scrolls. The simple devotee, with no outward sign of learning, can sometimes know more than the clever sage with his shimmering personality of other men's sayings. Yesod is the reflection of all that has gone before. The lower paths focus here. It is all that a man has acquired, though it will take time for it to become really his own. Yesod is a reflection of his philosophy or religion by the light he allows to shine down from Tiferet. In Yesod he sees himself as if in a mirror until, one day, he sees that he can view directly from Tiferet his own essential nature.

Yesod is the Moon and its metal is silver. Tiferet is the Sun and its metal is gold. Herein lies the wealth of a man.

Malkhut, for both finance and philosophy, is the kingdom of the elements. For the financier it is the world of substance and energy out of which he builds his artifact kingdom. Constructing and destroying he moulds the planet's surface, sometimes beautifully, sometimes badly. He works, though he may not be aware of it, under the eye of a great intelligence. He may tame Nature but he is never her master. Man reaches out to the upper air and even the Moon but he is still a child of the planet Earth and must obey its laws. He can convert every stick and stone into a new form but he will not make the volume of the Earth greater. He may release energy as he pleases but it will be no more than was there. Here is Malkhut. The wealth of the Earth is waiting to be refined and, though the financier, industrialist, and worker may not realise it, they each contribute more to the evolution of the planet than the pollution of it. A million years of man's presence

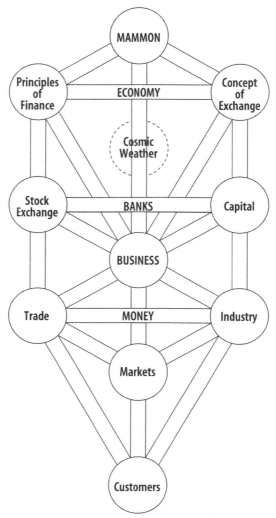

*Figure 37—ECONOMICS*
*This Tree shows how the balance of an economy operates with the left pillar as the structure and the right as the dynamic element. The central column indicates the state of the financial situation. This can fluctuate according to the law of supply and demand. Also, as noted, an economy can be influenced by the Solar and planetary conditions. Trade usually does well when there are plenty of sunspots which appear to stimulate human activity. The planets, when in harmonious configuration, generate a sense of confidence and sometimes stimulate conversely a mass migration when the economy is at the bottom of a cycle. This cosmic factor was considered in the medieval period. No major enterprise was begun without consulting a good astrologer.* (Halevi).

has indeed changed the face of the planet and this is part of its natural development in order to make it a more intelligent member of the Solar system. Through industry and technology men have landed on the Moon.

For the philosopher, Malkhut is his terrestrial body. This is his Earth, his Water, Air and Fire. Here is his vehicle, his chariot pulled by the vital vegetable forces, with himself as the charioteer and sometimes as the deputy master. Malkhut, to the religious man, is the temporary sojourn in the physical world. In this earthly shell he must reside, learning what lessons he can to refine his soul, until it drops from him and returns back to the earth to be recycled via the worms into another growth. The Kabbalist sees Malkhut as the residue of Creation, the densest yet richest of materialities. In this apparently solid world he knows all the higher ones are hidden. Indeed they are fully present, every one interwoven or overlaid and permeating through the Kingdom. Split an atom and Keter is there. Dissect a cell and Keter is there. Look at a living man, deep within the densest bone and inside the most complex centre of the brain — Keter is there — and more. The Absolute is omnipotent.

*Figure 38—LOVERS*

*Although falling in love seems very personal it is, in fact, a universal phenomenon. Mother Nature requires every species to produce offspring and humanity is no exception. At puberty, girls and boys become interested in sex as their bodies become adult. There is, however, another level to courtship; that of the soul. In Paradise, also called the Treasure House of Souls, each androgynous human spirit is split into male and female soul mates. While incarnate, each half of the psyche seeks to find its partner. However, this cannot occur until they heave learned many lessons in order to carry out their mutual spiritual destiny.* (Medieval image).

# 13. Love Affair

The human race is a complete Tree of Life with the male and female pillars demonstrating the relationship between the sexes. However, each person contains a complete Tree in miniature with the elements of active and passive present in both men and women. In the action of courtship the interplay of the two great cosmic laws show themselves well in the unfolding of a mutual octave between two people drawn together by a third force. So here we will study one of mankind's favourite tales and observe, with our theory and practice, the phenomenon of Love.

Setting the party scene with an old song's romantic but often quite accurate description of the opening event, a man and a girl see each other across a crowded room. Beginning in Malkhut, the hot smoky dimness was filled with jostling and dancing bodies. Talk and laughter abounded and the air was pervaded with the smell of sweat and perfume. Our couple noticed each other quite early in the evening; the man initially attracted by the girl's fair hair, the girl by the intelligent strength of his face. They observed each other surreptitiously at first, their Hods gleaning information, not only by their senses but in questioning the hostess and host about each other. The man found out her name, what she did and that she was unattached while his Nezah, aroused by the way she dressed, provoked a Yesodic image of what might lie beneath. She reminded him of an old love and he could not help superimposing the memory on the girl, especially when he discovered that their names were identical. The girl in her inquiry found that the man was unmarried, also that he was an architect. She was impressed for he not only had charm but respectable status. She suppressed the stupid idea that her parents would approve as her Yesod placed him in the context of her home. Intrigued, she waited for him to approach as she instinctively acknowledged the signals of interest focused in her direction. The lower great physical triads of both their Trees were now tuned up for action.

The hostess, quickly perceiving the situation, introduced them and then left. With the goddess Venus only too present they both overlaid the mutual attraction with nervous small talk, each hiding behind their party personas. By his accent she discovered he was an American. By hers, he guessed she came from a middle-class English family. As their Hods discussed mutual acquaintances and friends both scrutinised each other. She liked the back of his neck and his voice. His eyes wandered over her body. She was also intelligent and well read, just his type. She asked him about his work. He said he was in practice with three other young architects and they were just beginning to make headway on their first big project of designing a school. She listened attentively, observing his hands and the liveliness of his eyes. She was very drawn to him. He was so different from the well-mannered fops she had been used to. His slightly battered looks quite aroused her.

Suddenly he said the noise of the party was unbearable. Would she like to slip out for some fresh air? To her own surprise she agreed without her usual obstruction to such a proposition. The party had become a bore, she rationalised, as they made their way through the dancers.

Walking down the street they were both strangely silent under the inner tension. He was reconsidering his standard method by which he got girls into bed. It was somehow inapplicable for there was an unnerving element present in the sense of already knowing what would happen, though why he should think this he could not fathom. She was confused. Normally she did not allow herself to be so easily isolated from a party where she had been safe with her friends. Here she was with a complete stranger. Or was she? The question was odd for she felt she had met him before, though where she could not tell.

He began, English style, to talk about the weather and soon they were comparing their respective countries' climates and seasonal conditions in the cities of New York and London. All through this pointless conversation there was another, a Hod, Nezah, Yesod and Malkhut dialogue going on. It was in the touch of his hand on her arm and her response in the question and answer game of the sexes. The tension increased as they approached her small flat. She wanted to invite him in but her judgement (Gevurah) said no. It was too early in the evening and too soon. Her upbringing and her image of herself would not allow it, she told herself. He, detecting her hesitance, did not press her and suggested they walk on. She was relieved and moved by this sensitive response to her resistance. Maybe, she thought as they passed her front door, she would not object to being seduced. Suddenly energy that came from she knew not where flowed through her limbs and, taking his offered hand, she accepted and gave the first kiss. From that moment on they were both in another realm (the animal triad). Abruptly there was no darkness. The Moon emerged as if from nowhere and the stars appeared to be twice as bright in a deep vast sky. Everything about them, even the buildings, seemed alive and full of colour. They saw, as they walked arms about each other, with such clarity, heard and smelt with such acuteness, that every street was filled with an extraordinary magic. With both functional sides of the Tree excited, the triad of self-consciousness was stimulated.

They wandered for miles and talked the hours away. By two in the morning they had covered each other's entire personal history and knew all there was to know in words. At his front door she assented to the suggestion that she would like a coffee before going home. As they climbed the stair in a dreamlike haze, the air became charged with passion.

The coffee was made but not drunk. A deeper hunger had taken command. Gradually undressing, each explored the other's body, not only for pleasure but in an unconscious instinctive probing to see that every part was normal. Naked, they enjoyed all their senses, each touch, smell and taste adding to the inner heightening of bodily sensations and feelings. In bed, close in embrace, their minds fluctuated between passing thought and complete silence: Hod, Nezah, and Malkhut. There was little talk, the only communication being touch, sight and sound. Yesodic dreams continually clouded their brains, separating them, as romanticised imagery was projected onto the physical reality. His eye observed faults in her beauty but this was overlaid. She discerned flaws in his confidence. These thoughts, however, were ignored, washed away in the gentle passion she sensed building up within her body. Last night she had been alone and frustrated. Now she was elated, almost on the edge of release. Slowly the man drew her closer together, until their rhythms coincided. Nearer they approached, blending into single motion. Suddenly they were one and in the climax of ecstasy they met and dissolved into nothing, as they rose up the column of equilibrium from Tiferet to Daat. And Adam knew Eve.

Slowly out of the ecstatic void they emerged, separated, to become individuals, as gently they returned to their bodies again. Cloudy thoughts and feelings ebbed back but they could not drown the

136

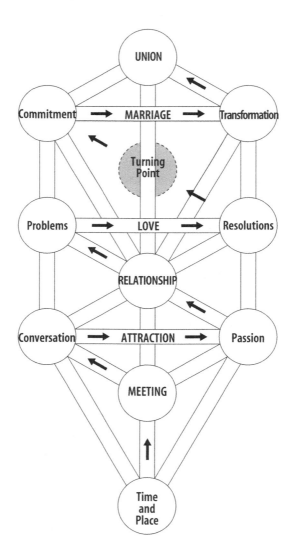

*Figure 39—COURTSHIP*
*A relationship usually begins with mutual attraction. It may be the recognition of one's soul mate or someone who represents them as their type. The latter connection maybe very short, as the deeper aspects of temperament and level reveal, 'This is not the one'. Most people settle for a partner who is the nearest to the unconscious memory of their past and future partner. This is because they still have much to learn about themselves and the art of relationships. If they met their soul mate before they were ready, passion could become an obsession and they would be quite useless to the universe. (Halevi).*

profound meeting they had experienced. Nothing could erase, not even the body's reverberating fatigue, that momentary yet timeless contact. Only that seemed real. They looked at each other in the dim light, seeing only a smiling face of skin and bone. True, the eyes still retained the consciousness but where was the person each had contacted, face to face? He touched her cheek and this was reassuring to both of them. From that point on, moment by moment, they descended into the world of ordinary living. In her, practical thoughts began to test romanticism. She had been caught once before by infatuation. And yet it was not the same. This was permeated through with a curious sense of knowing, of recognition. She sighed, exhausted in her pleasant fatigue. Never before had she felt so safe, even in the most familiar surroundings of her home.

He, in the limp ebb tide of his passion, lay thinking. This experience could only be matched by his first love of long ago on his uncle's New England farm. Without the smell of hay or larks overhead in the summer sky, he had relived one of the most moving experiences of his life. This was remarkable because he had had love affairs and all, in the light of this night, were shown up as mostly physical. It was a shock. He had not really known any of them. This girl was the first he had really seen as more than a woman.

They both lay silent for a long time, wondering what had happened. Here was no casual night passage. Something important had occurred. They had been joined for a brief instant and neither could ever forget that moment. Whatever happened in the relationship that was to follow, nothing could ever break this connection. Tiferet had met Tiferet.

By morning, however, enchantment had set in. The hard light of dawn and ordinary life called on sentiment and they constructed a romantic idyll to preserve the feeling of the night. Soon the original contact was lost as they sank into the self-enchanting games lovers play. Yesod had re-established itself.

Over the ensuing weeks the idyll bore them on exotic wings, changing every place and time they met into a fairyland. Affection grew in shared experience and gradually, as the honeymoon phase faded, a quite genuine love between them was generated. But something new began to appear with the raising of Gevurah. Mutual criticism began to emerge. At first silent, it developed into occasional irritation as they began to examine the image each had imposed on the other. This led on to comment, then bickering when they saw their idol dissolve into human weakness. At times there was open quarrelling

138

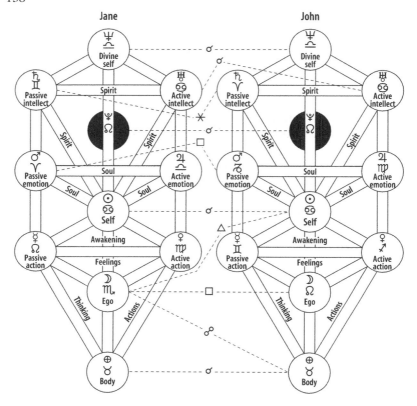

*Figure 40—ROMANCE*

*Here John and Jane meet at a party. They are physically attracted because they both have Taurus on the Ascendant. However, his flamboyant Leo Moon, being squared to her probing Scorpio Moon, stimulates a certain irritation. Even so, they both have Cancerian Selves and so they relate at the deeper level of the soul and the lesser level of the body while their egos quarrel over personal trivia. Meanwhile, his Watery Sun would relate to her Watery Moon as an elder brother while she might, in spite of her reservation, see him as a father figure. Alas, their squared Marses are incompatible and their affair might end in a violent emotional drama. (Halevi).*

when one refused to conform to the other's dream. He found her possessive and demanding and she discovered he was extremely moody. Occasionally exchanges were sharp and belligerent, only to be dissolved on the bed of Venus where Mars was placated.

By the sixth month of their relationship they reached a turning point. The tinsel novelty had gone but they felt strongly enough about each other to consider living together. This had precipitated an unexpected crisis. While they agreed that running two flats and one love affair was inconvenient, both also shared the view of remaining independent. In this lay the rub. Such trial marriages were not uncommon in their circle but there was also the question of property and territory which revealed a crucial issue. When it came to signing the lease for the apartment whose place would it be? Each discovered a strong sense of ego. Neither of their Yesods would step down to be the tenant partner. Both wished to be the retaining landlord, should they eventually split up. Each saw themselves as sacrificing their integrity for the convenience of the other. A row actually developed outside the estate office. He felt his masculinity insulted, she her security threatened. Maybe they had better part now, they concluded. It was obvious that each of them was completely selfish and totally incompatible.

That night in bed, after a miserable evening in her place, the miraculous happened again. At the climax of making love, now a pleasurable routine, the Tiferet connection made on their first night was re-established. Suddenly they were one again. Perhaps only for a second but long enough to see there was a deep bond between them. Here Hesed was touched upon. Abruptly, all the conflicts became trivial in the radiance of this expansive inner emotion. Everything suddenly was forgiven and all real or imagined hurts were forgotten. Their egos retreated, became magnanimous, each allowing the other to exist in its own right. They saw that their relationship could go on but with each person developing separately.

Time tested their relationship and they gradually grew to respect and understand one another as the faculties of Binah slowly came into operation. They had their periods of difficulty, particularly when she saw friends have children or his work went through a bad period. Occasionally even their intimacy became stale and they indeed argued like a married couple, each knowing by now the other's habits and attitudes. Their second major crisis came when they realised they could go no further. They must change the half-completed relationship or separate. Neither wished to move and so they both embarked on a series of disastrous love affairs elsewhere.

Within two months they had returned to each other, both recognising in the pain of their experiences that they much preferred each other. This was seen in a flash one night as their reunion not only reminded them of all they had shared but showed them, by the past pattern, all that was possible for the future. Here Binah connected with Hokhmah, illuminating the obvious fact that they were designed for each other, foibles and all. Daat completed the self-evident realisation with its extraordinary certainty and they decided they had no other choice but to marry. The Tree of their relationship was all but finished.

At the wedding a curious event occurred. When the minister carried out the ceremony both the man and the woman perceived, during the rite, a subtle joining within them. It was as if something from above confirmed their union. Moreover, as the bride turned to the groom she suddenly knew that on first sight she had unconsciously recognised her husband.

Our story is perhaps a classic situation, for it contains the principle of mutual growth and balance in the respective Trees of each partner. It also demonstrates the kabbalistic tradition related to men and women wherein the intimate connection is a direct analogue of the Tree and the meeting of Heaven and Earth. Marriage, a real union and not merely a legal arrangement, is rare because in most people one or more sefirot are not working correctly. An active Gevurah is a common reason for shrewish wives and an unbalanced Nezah-Hod relationship has wrecked many marriages, while a masking Yesod of lies has outwardly preserved more than one marital disaster.

Sex is both a cosmic and personal activity. The cosmic is to produce offspring while the personal allows two individuals to connect at various levels. These can be physical, psychological and spiritual. For most people it is either one or two of the lower. The union of all three is a rarity.

# 14. Birth-Life-Death

Continuing the story from the last chapter we examine two Trees resulting from the conception of a child. The first is concerned with its gestation and birth, the second with its subsequent process on entering the world outside the womb with its growth and death. Here we study descending and ascending octaves.

Our couple, now married, decide to have a child—or Fate, whatever this strange element might be, places them in a situation where a child is conceived. Seen from the point of view of the Tree, Hokhmah is the Father and Binah is the Mother and when they come together, united in Yesod, and if the conditions are right, that is, that the column of equilibrium is charged with creation, conception occurs. From the father comes the active principle, all the male attributes of him, his family and race. From Binah the same contributions are made with the feminine elements added. Here the dynamic is formulated, the history of two lines of generation woven in the dance of the chromosomes. The sex of the child is probably determined in Binah, as is its dark or light hair, tendency to grow tall or small and have a weak or strong chest. If we suppose the father is Jewish and the mother English we get a blend of the ethnic characteristics which in life will give the child an insight and understanding of two outlooks. He may be volatile and practical or phlegmatic yet shrewd. Dozens of combinations are possible on this level. In Binah also is the probable setting of all the clocks, both biological and spiritual, as well as the general temperament.

After conception the Lightning Flash passes on to Hesed. Here begins the process of organic expansion and growth. Within a matter of days the fertilised ovum has divided into a number of cells and formed into a hollow ball. This mass continues to expand at an extraordinary rate until, fed by nutrient obtained from the wall of the mother's womb, it has become an embryonic disc. At this point the Gevurah principle at work in gestation begins with the differentiation of the cells into various functions, the chief of which is the formation

142

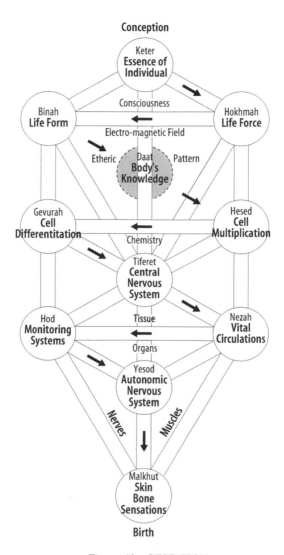

Conception

Keter
**Essence of
Individual**

Binah
**Life Form**

Consciousness

Hokhmah
**Life Force**

Electro-magnetic Field

Etheric    Daat    Pattern
**Body's
Knowledge**

Gevurah
**Cell
Differentitation**

Chemistry

Hesed
**Cell
Multiplication**

Tiferet
**Central
Nervous
System**

Hod
**Monitoring
Systems**

Tissue

Organs

Nezah
**Vital
Circulations**

Yesod
**Autonomic
Nervous
System**

Nerves    Muscles

Malkhut
**Skin
Bone
Sensations**

Birth

*Figure 41—GESTATION*

*Conception occurs when the Creative World of the spirit joins with the centre of the Tree of the psyche and the Crown of the body. This means a discarnate soul is ready to return to Earth to learn its next lesson. In this Tree the psychical process is managed by Mother Nature who has spent millions of years perfecting the human body through evolution. As the embryo grows so the soul becomes increasingly involved in physicality. The moment of birth locks the psyche into the fleshy vehicle. In the Bible this is called putting on a 'coat of skin'. The notion of reincarnation is accepted in the Kabbalah and is known as the* Gilgulim, the Wheels of Life. *(Halevi).*

into specialist roles of three cell layers. These are the entoderm, which becomes the inmost systems of digestion and its associated function; the mesoderm which produces the middle zone of muscles, bones and connective tissue; and the ectoderm which forms eventually into the outer skin, the brain and spinal column. The Gevurah differentiation takes place when the embryonic disc is still less than an eighth of an inch in diameter.

From this time on Hesed and Gevurah work together, Hesed producing growth, Gevurah defining and determining organs and functions. In the ectoderm the head begins to form, the nervous system is laid out and the lenses of the eyes are resolved. For the mesoderm the different muscles and bones are focused with the lungs, alimentary canal, sex and blood rapidly evolving; while the entoderm lines the breathing passage, alimentary canal and bladder. This interbalanced labour goes on in correct sequence governed by the plan in Binah and generated by the creative impulse begun in Hokhmah.

Tiferet announces the presence of the essential nature. By its position on the Lightning Flash it would imply that when the embryo is whole, the particular intelligence imbued by the central column of consciousness, headed by Keter and focus of the four previous sefirot, arrives.

Here it waits, during the period of gestation, for birth; though in the case of miscarriage or abortion it may, as the Hebrew prayer book says, 'pass by the world without entering it'.

The gestation process continues with Nezah not only setting all the biological rhythms and cycles of blood, digestion etc. in motion but also in installing the principle of conservation, so that there is a continuous renewal, be it of cells, the instinct of self-preservation or of regeneration of the species in the desire for sex. This Nezah principle applies right through, not only in the organism but in the person's psyche which continually seeks conducive habits that preserve his sense of wellbeing. While the embryo is still connected to the mother and participates in her circulation, its desire to survive is very present and communicates itself through the Nezah in the mother, whose lethargic state is designed to obviate any personal erratic behaviour. She is under the rulership of Venus and the Moon, the twin godmothers of Nature.

Hod might be called here the harmonising principle. Not only are various sensory organs completed by the Hodian nervous systems but the whole organism is tuned within the limiting defines of Gevurah

144

*Figure 42 — BIRTH*
*Everyone is born at a specific time and place, to a particular family, in a certain historic period. This is the law of karma, known in Kabbalah as 'Measure for Measure'. The moment of incarnation is part of a cosmic process in which the microcosm of the psyche resonates with the celestial macrocosm. The birth chart on the astrologer's table gives the horoscope settings of resonance to which that particular person will respond. For example, a strong Mars in a chart will actively resonate when the planet conjoins with its natal position. Fate is the life pattern based upon performance in previous lives. The current incarnation is designed to give the maximum opportunity to develop, if the person chooses to.* (16th century woodcut).

into a highly responsive instrument. Hod permeates the embryo, passing data back and forth so that the preceding processes are brought into fine adjustment. To illustrate its function in a negative way; when a group of cells is not in sympathy with the tuning of the organism as a whole, cancer may occur and an unbalanced Nezah will supply it with nutrient and maintain the malignant growth. Unless Gevurah is informed and all the data passed on to the related sefirot, the tumour will expand and destroy its benefactor body and subsequently itself, so selfish is its orientation. Hod makes it possible for the body to perceive what is going on. By its ability to scan, it can learn of the slightest aberration then inform Nezah, for example, to send out white blood corpuscles to counter infection in the system. Acting as the balance to Nezah, Hod also looks outwards through the senses to monitor the environment. This is even at work in the womb when the child kicks until it finds itself a more comfortable position.

Yesod in this case is the personality of the whole organism, as yet unimpressed by the outside world. It sits in the middle of the Hod-Nezah-Malkhut triad, the modelled but smooth wax of the brain, body and psyche of the child. Like a mirror it is made in a certain way, perhaps clear, maybe misty, even distorted, depending on what occurred before during gestation. It carries no memories, only built-in characteristics, flaws and foibles. A family gift for music is perhaps latent or a tendency to violence; maybe also an aptitude for mechanics or an inherent dislike for high places. Not active, these things, created by a combination of the particular balance of the sefirot, may lie dormant throughout life until brought out by stress or some conducive circumstance. A Mozart in a mining village would perhaps never get beyond the chapel organ while a mechanical genius could well be wasting his time playing in the London Philharmonic Orchestra, never having time in the rush of a professional musician's life to take up his hobby of inventing gadgets. Yesod might loosely be called the mind, the ordinary mind, and we shall explore it further when we take the Tree in the opposite direction from birth to death.

Malkhut, the Kingdom of the Elements, is the physical body. All the other sefirot supply the energy and form which create the physical organism we see emerging from the womb. From Yesod upwards there are principles, like the desire for survival. They are manifest through the body but it itself is merely a vehicle, an ever-changing aggregate of cells of which only the brain tissue has anything approaching the length of life of the man himself, for many cells last merely a day or so, others at most a few weeks. We are a continually changing standing wave, as science calls such a phenomenon. The only apparently permanent elements are the workings of the sefirot which maintain our consciousness, form and energy while increasing the body's size up to maturity before the exhausted organism, no longer capable of supporting cellular life, collapses at death. It is interesting to repeat from Genesis the idea that we have fallen or descended into coats of skins, that we are bound by the laws of organic life, denied for a period the upper garden of Eden. On conception we are imprisoned in a physical form and then ejected from the womb of Eve into the natural kingdom from where we begin on birth the octave of return.

At birth we take our first breath. With this sudden jolt a child is severed from its mother at the end of a creative octave and becomes an independent being. Anyone witnessing a birth knows the sense of profound impact, not only on themselves but particularly on the baby which reacts in a definite way to its entry into our dimension. Some arrivals do not wish to embark on the journey and are stillborn, others prefer to hold back until they are dragged in by a slap on the back. Others fight the shock of being removed from the protection of the womb, while yet others accept they are here, at least for a while. This initial period is sometimes called the 'Age of Wisdom'—a curious name more suited to the end of life, yet from another view birth and death are the same place. Therefore this name may well be valid. However, no baby as yet has the vocabulary to explain its experience but then this is equally true of mystics just emerging from ecstasy, so we are left with the wondrous impression of the baby's awakening into our world, followed by its Hod-Nezah yell for warmth and food as the two side pillars of function come into full independent action.

Malkhut is the wet and living body of the baby. From this moment on it begins its journey back to Keter containing the whole Tree, as Keter is in Malkhut, but this Tree will not perhaps be seen outwardly, except over the years as the person grows back up it again. The first stage is the path between Malkhut and Yesod—babyhood. In this period not only is the body rapidly increasing its volume but it is also soaking up internal and external information. From Hod it absorbs through its senses the smells, sounds, tastes, and sights of its mother. Touch is perhaps the most important sensor with temperature and comfort playing an important part in forming its world image in Yesod. Nezah adds to the picture, the baby slowly recognising the daily rhythm and response of the parent who comes running to its every call. Later, as the Yesodic image is extended beyond intimate bodily exploration and reaction to internal cycles, the baby begins to push out its sensory field, throwing things from its bed as part of the programme for studying height and distance. By the beginning of childhood (each sefirotic stage blends into the next) the baby has begun to control its functions, walk and speak, developing the faculties of physical Hod.

The period of Hod is the time when the child learns about everything around it. Always curious, it questions and explores continuously the local geography of its home and the intellectual world opened up by reading and the media. Boyhood is occupied with experimentation, ranging from seeing how much weight a tree branch can take to simple chemistry. Museums are a favourite place and so are any holes or caves. Vast collections of fascinating junk are accumulated and an endless inquiry into the biggest, strongest, longest and heaviest things and creatures on the Earth are conducted. This surely is the sefirah of Mercury with its chameleon range of interests, including tricks, deception and even thievery—as any orchard owner knows! Speed and lightness are all-important and the agility displayed in the school playground is self evident, as is the cacophony of young, high-pitched, mercurial voices. As adolescence approaches the child has a very clear world-picture. Its persona is now well formed, its education covering over its essential nature, sometimes so much so that it blocks out the light. This is well demonstrated by the English public school system which can overlay a boy's true nature with such a strongly conventional social mask that often it imprisons him for life. Admirable as a tool in service to a man's real self, the persona is a bad master if there is to be any real development. As frequently observed, many people do not free themselves beyond Yesod and Hod, preferring to eat, drink and talk in old clichés and habits picked up at school. In life their values are governed by gratification or impressionability, their desires often directed by people who have the determination of Gevurah, the power of Tiferet or the desire of Nezah. This may appear somewhat scathing but the Western world in particular runs its commerce on the evocation of these weaknesses and dominances.

Youth is the time of Nezah. With it comes the awareness of beauty and love. Girls grow conscious of their bodies and boys of the rising of passion. It is the age of Venus, a time to wear the latest becoming style, know the current musical hit, pass through all the sweet intrigues of romance in a pleasant world of poetry. This is the time of

148

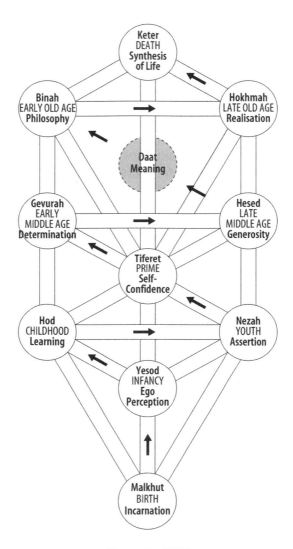

*Figure 43—LIFE*
*Here the return impulse is shown in the unfolding or the octave of birth to death. This process may not always be fulfilled as many die, for example, from drink or for karmic reasons before their time. Even so, the classic stages of growth, maturity and decay bear witness to the sefirotic pattern. However, psychologically some people can sometimes get no further than childhood. Others can likewise fixate at youth, behaving like teenagers at the age of sixty. Most people reach maturity but do not go on to develop their soul and spirit. Only the great saints and sages complete the ascent but the way is open to all who wish to become SELF-realised. (Halevi).*

flower children and endless unexpected pregnancies. Here is a daydreamer's realm, recognisable in *Romeo and Juliet* and *West Side Story*. Energy and ease, ebb and flow as courtship passes through the cycle of seduction, orgasm and relaxation. Here is Nezah or Eternity with the continuous round of love passing from partner to partner in a long chain of embraces. The world is rosy. Youth has no sorrows other than that of unrequited affection and there is always another beloved to fill that heartache. Pain, illness and death have no place here, everyone is vital and beautiful without a trace of rheumatism. To sleep out of doors is fun, to sing to the guitar till dawn no physical problem. Fatigue is quickly washed away by love and the body's waxing strength can take any punishment. This is the age when the boy and the girl separate from home, the intimacy of love projecting them into the first sense of independence. This is the spring before the full flowering of a man or woman.

Tiferet is the prime of life. At this point Nature has reached her zenith. She has endowed all that organic life can impart and the essential nature has at its command all the physical equipment it might need. Many great works of art are created during this age and men often come into their own at this time if they have progressed beyond Nezah. Those who have not still amuse themselves with love affairs and pleasures far beyond their years, hoping to retain a youth since gone. Modern advertising exploits this, convincing the mature that the physical qualities of youth have more to offer than the intelligence of their own experience. Men and women who are bodily-oriented forget the possibilities of their souls and strive to remain young till even the most expensive makeovers cannot hide the loss of youth. Organic time cannot be frozen.

The age of Tiferet is unique because, lying on the central axis of consciousness, it opens access to inner development. While Yesod supplies awareness of the outer world and Hod and Nezah perform their functions, Tiferet opens the gate to immortality. Through the true self-consciousness of a man, with a fully operative and well-running machine, it is possible for him to see, at this physical peak, the nature of his whole life. At this point he can know where his career lies, can foresee a direction to be taken. Tiferet enables him to decide at the mid-point of his life whether he chooses or is made to choose. Here a man has the power to be himself. He may be a servant of a large company but he can be himself, have his own integrity and individuality. Certainly the temptation of ego is present but this at

*Figure 44—SOUL GROUPS*
*Each person is a member of a unit that relates to a part of Adam Kadmon. They move through time together, although not always in the same blood line. They begin their incarnation often in the same family but later disperse in order to widen their development. Later, they unite as soul mates and meet up with others to become a group of artists, scientists or explorers. History is full of such examples in the Greek philosophers, medieval saints and even revolutionaries who move humanity on, as did those who began the Renaissance. In this drawing is a soul group associated with Law. In some cases, it can be a rabbinic line or a military family.* (Sir Thomas More's household, Holbein, 16th century).

least indicates that a man has matured and the remedy is inherent. A villain has more possibility of growth than a shadow of a man who lives through only his Yesod which is sometimes no more than a collection of imitations acquired, borrowed and stolen from other men.

Gevurah is the period of determination. It could be called manhood, that is, when the power of the full stature is applied to a direction. Taking the symbol of Mars we can see the hallmark of a man who has reached this level and age. He could be a company director or an artist working along his own original line. There is courage present and discrimination. He does not deviate, except to adjust to problems that are probably more learning situations than fences to be jumped *en route* to his ambition. There is an emotional element in his work. He continues to labour just for interest where lesser men only work for money. Something drives him. It may be that he wants a better home or to give his children a good education. Whatever it is, it gives him a surety and a decisiveness that marks him out. Negatively it can make him aggressive, the ruthless careerist who will tread on anybody who gets in his way. His motivation may be power, as the Hod-Tiferet-Gevurah triad, untempered by a strong balancing Hesed-Nezah-Tiferet triad, drives him on. Conversely he can, with this level of judgement, discriminate finely, have an eye for situations, products and people that makes employers want him as their servant. Such a man is invaluable in a negotiating team as an expert and this, again, will single him out as a man with a definite skill and knowledge that is his very own. Manhood is reached by few men as real masters, though some are forced superficially to act the part in order to compete and dominate. This is external pressure and not true to a person's inner nature. In time such a man wonders whether it was worth the effort when younger men replace him. When our man reaches the point where he goes it alone, takes a decision, perhaps against advice or even common sense, to follow his own star, we can say he has reached the Gevurah initiation.

The period of Hesed is middle age. This is perhaps after the tough long haul of bringing up a family or that part of a career which separates the professional from the amateur. By this time a man has a wealth of experience, maybe the material goods, too, that go with this age. He possesses most of the things he desired—perhaps success, personal satisfaction, even outworn delusion. He has reached a point where the pressure can be relaxed. He is more tolerant, more benign. Certainly

*Figure 45—DEATH*
*Is this the end, just a few bones? Even the most primitive cultures believed there was life after death and buried objects with the body for use in their versions of afterlife. Some societies burned their dead to aid the soul's release from Earthly shackles. Not a few believed that they could still communicate with the deceased. In the kabbalistic tradition, the 'Next World' refers not only to immortality but to the next life. This is in the prayers which speak of God 'quickening' the dead. All is not lost upon dying. The good and bad deeds, emotions and thoughts of a person are still carried by the discarnate psyche to the appropriate invisible level of rest and reflection before the prenatal stage of reincarnation. (Woodcut, 16th century).*

he works hard but not with the same verve. This is not only because his physical powers are beginning to wane but also because, with his expanded view, he can see the best way to accomplish an operation. He sees that rapid action and determination have their place, and that younger men can fulfill this better than he can, but he also sees the overspill of a scheme, the ramifications he could not see while his view was limited. Life becomes more pleasant; work is important but he can afford to relax, be generous. He is, if the desire to work is still strong, more inclined to look at his industry on a grander scale. Money or status is no longer the consideration. There is a certain joy in what he does. He may even become suddenly benevolent and socially conscience-stricken, want to help the poor as the American millionaire Peabody did or even start philanthropic foundations like Ford and Rockefeller. If he is a loner, perhaps an artist, and he has really matured far beyond the Gevurah competitive age, he may wish to help younger painters or writers as T. S. Eliot did. This is indeed the age of the Jovial, as the Martial was of the Gevurah period.

Between Hesed and Binah lies the invisible sefirah of Daat. This is the point in a man's life when he really knows what it has all been about. If he has evolved this far—and most people do not because they prefer to remain in the illusion of their most pleasant time, usually their youth—an evolved man will relate all he has learnt to the pattern of his life. From this position, directly above Tiferet, he will be able to look back and see with knowing eyes all the winding paths he trod. This will lead him to a deep realisation that life is a game in which the art is to participate but not be caught. The world is literally a stage and a man's life is a walk-on part. He will recognise this and observe with cynicism or humour, depending on how he arrived at the view, that there is a second birth to undergo before death. In many who reach this conclusion the void of Daat, or the disappearance of the ego, may be too much. In death they know they must give up all their worldly gains but they hold on, clinging to memories and possessions, avoiding the second great shock and potential birth since they entered the world. Those who see this point as an opportunity begin to retire from the world before they are forced to leave it by death. They may continue to work in the world but their attitude is not of it. In the Indian tradition a householder hands over to his sons all his worldly duties and retires. In the West a man may do the same but join a golf club. However, even in the technological societies of Europe and North America there are some who follow the same idea of spiritual retirement and it is important to remember that a person can arrive at this point at any time. Many a remarkable man has made his fortune before forty and devoted the rest of his life to personal evolution, be it joining a monastery or, like Schliemann the German millionaire, devoting it to archaeology. This critical change brings us to Binah.

Binah is old age. Contrary to the usual belief that this period is a terminal one of running down, it is the preparation for the dynamic of death. Certainly the body is decaying and all the vital processes are sluggish but the invisible part of man that inhabits this physical shell is, or should be, full of a lifetime's experience. While the body can no longer run a mile, usually an unnecessary accomplishment in old age, the soul can ponder on the material collected over the years. Silence and stillness are all that are needed. A good head and heart, backed up by a slowly clearing memory of earlier times so characteristic of old age, can review life and come to an understanding not possible in a busy outward existence. Time is the quality of Binah, whose traditional planet is Saturn. Here is the ability to survey decades, see the links and knots of years, use the knowledge of Daat to unravel mysteries of fate in hindsight, see how certain meetings and partings were fatal, perceive that particular situations taught precisely the needed lesson. A whole library of intimate films can be replayed without the pressing desires, value judgement or over-indulgent assessments. Scenes can be relived with greater clarity, the true facts about situations learned years later, piecing together the unknown. Here at Binah, in the Winter of physical life, is the possibility of sensing the next Spring. Laid out is a whole life-year with all its seasons. In the closing in of the senses the inner world becomes more real, the invisible realm closer. Childhood memories return, smells and sights recalled that were long forgotten. Old faces, even the dead, constantly visit the contemplator and behind them are intimations of Paradise. To the unthinking this appears to be the point of departure, to the thoughtful it is an approaching. Here is the leap across the Tree to Hokhmah. Those who reach old age and are still spiritually undeveloped see the reversed jump of the Lightning Flash as the blinding light of obliterating death. To those who have understood the meaning of their lives through Binah and Daat, death is perceived quite differently. They glimpse through the curtain of Hokhmah a bright world beyond. In the silent, deep thought of the inner intellect, illumination comes not to frighten, as death does the unprepared, but to illuminate the path back to Keter—the Crown. In Hokhmah is the wisdom of a lifetime flashing down the years through all the sefirot to Malkhut. As death separates the soul of a man from his coat of skin and draws him up into the next world, those present at his death will recognise that a cosmic event has taken place. Indeed, so potent is this occurrence that its impact is felt often over a great distance and for many years. This is the power of Hokhmah, in death as profound an insight as for those who witness a birth.

In Keter is the end and the beginning. It is the open Crown through which the spirit enters and departs, sometimes to come and at others to return.

# 15. Time

Having looked at birth and death, let us use the Tree in a quite different way to examine Time. First we must realise that there are different orders of Time. The method of using a clock, be it a twenty-four-hour or a microsecond meter, is more convenient than accurate. The Sun, for instance, for most of the year arrives at the noon meridian early or late and the time, according to the stars, has to be continually adjusted to make a scientific constant. So we must leave the common understanding of time alone.

The most familiar form of Time we know—that is for human beings, for every creature has its own measure—is what is called Passing Time. This is seen on the screen of Yesod which views the world of Malkhut as a passing show, a continuous stream of images focusing and dissolving in between the inner day-dreams. At night, when the path between Yesod and Malkhut is shut down, the daydreams come to the forefront like stars at night and Time appears to do strange things. This Passing Time is the one we generally regard as real and correlate to the clock. This is an illusion and quite unreliable, as the contrast between a boring or an interesting day will tell you by the way the hours drag in one and go too swiftly in the other. It is apparent, from a little thought and observation, that the clock measures nothing of our personal life, though it is useful for arranging meetings and other external practical matters. As for our real sense of time our watch is useless. The young man waiting for his girl finds ten minutes intolerably long and the parting kiss unbearably short for quite different subjective reasons. This is the result of the interaction of different levels and dimensions of Time.

Man is a Tree of Life and each sefirah has its own time scale. If we take Tiferet as a day and night, the essence of Time, we see a complete cycle around which the various clocks of the Tree function. In Tiferet is a conscious measure. A man can take in a whole day, his being can perceive it as one piece. Time in the other sefirot is either too long or too short to grasp in entirety but a day is comprehensible by his body and soul.

Normally a man sees the world through Yesodic time. He views the passage of events, imagining them to be real but when he suddenly wakes up, perhaps in the middle of a car accident, everything changes. Often the most memorable characteristic of such an event is that time appears to slow down. Perhaps, while out driving a pedestrian slips in front of him. He catches sight of the fall and sees the whole action quite clearly in a fraction of a clock second, yet he takes in more in that instant than he saw in a whole day of Yesodic time. He swerves, brakes his car and watches it apparently drift slowly into collision with a lamp post. His body, however, working on another time scale, cannot respond fast enough to correct the skid. It seems to be extraordinarily sluggish even though he knows his reflexes are incredibly fast. He observes the situation unfold gradually before his eyes, the curiously impartial watcher within himself suddenly alerted. He follows the action as if he were viewing a slowed-down film frame by frame. Some sportsmen know this phenomenon well and see a cricket or baseball approach them more like a slow-moving balloon than an express train. This is the Hod view of Time which sees Time in infinitesimal impressions or reverberations. They can be as short as a one ten-thousandth of a second. One of these impressions can freeze a tiny event into a readable picture for the mind. Our memories are full of such instances. Nor should it be rare, for our nervous and sensory systems are based on this high-frequency response. Hod's highest range of frequency is our shortest impression, or one fine electric spark in length. Looking through Hod's timescale, a minute is made up of thousands of such flashes. If it were not so the eye could not function, though to our normal sensibility these ever-changing images blend into the continuous flow called sight.

It is possible to heighten our sensibility so as to appear to slow down Hod's time at will. This can be done unnaturally with drugs like LSD but not only is this unlawful in a spiritual sense, it is as dangerous as putting rocket fuel in a small car. It will go fast for a while, then burn it out—for ever. The lawful way is to acquire this consciousness by intelligent and diligent cultivation. The Arts are one means of attaining it, as many painters demonstrate with their frozen moments on canvas and many composers attempt to evoke such an acute state with their music. The cinema recognises the dramatic impact of slowing time down. For those who practise a spiritual discipline this phenomenon is familiar. Here is one of the gates to higher consciousness. In the alert state that comes with, for instance, a meditation practice, a nod

158

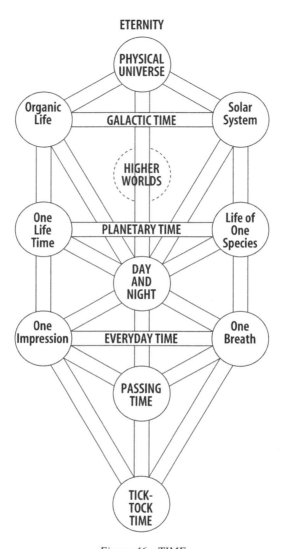

*Figure 46—TIME*
In this Tree, degrees of time are set out. Time is essentially movement against the
backdrop of Eternity. The tick-tock time of a clock is one but a crude mechanical
measure. In contrast, passing time can fluctuate according to one's moods. For example,
a fleeting impression can seem quite long if it is profound and in some cases can last
a lifetime. Day and night is a physical calibration, as is the Solar year. However, on
a larger scale, Time has different qualities. The life of a species is but a millisecond
to the Milky Way while the material universe is only a twinkle in the eye of the
Absolute. (Halevi).

or a single word can convey a whole statement in an instant. Only a sharp and well-tuned Hod could catch such a conversation. Perhaps a story will illustrate this dimension. An angel once appeared to a man one night. Naturally he was rather surprised and knocked over a jug. This was instantly forgotten as he was carried up through all the levels of the Heavenly Kingdom to the Foot of God Himself. After seeing all the celestial sights he was brought down through the Worlds and eventually returned to his bed, just in time to observe the jug he had knocked over hit the floor.

Nezah is a breath, that is, one complete cycle relating to the inner and outer world. The body is full of clocks, each with its own rhythm, the chief being the heart beat, but this does not directly connect with the world outside. A breath does and, in its rhythm, it partakes of both exterior and interior. This gives it a unique view, for it reveals a corresponding relationship. A moment of fright demonstrates this reciprocal reaction. Throughout a breath, in such a moment, the whole situation is taken in by the thousands of impressions flooding into the Hod faculty. By the end of that same breath they have been analysed and the Nezah autonomic system has adjusted the organism for flight or fight.

Anyone under the spell of love knows the moment to moment changes in mood and metabolism. The relationship is measured out in breaths, long or short, and the sequence extends like an ecstatic chain to the climax breath of orgasm. This link with the instinctive mind connects with Nature and sometimes a beautiful view literally takes the breath away. Here is an inherent response and it can be observed to act in sympathy at the turn of the evening or at dawn in a forest when the vegetable world reverses its oxygen-carbon dioxide respiration. At such a moment there is a distinct pause as the systole and diastole of Nature changes over. Nezah is the clock of breath, measuring out not just the instant of Hod but complete moments. These are not just impressions but a whole situation, be it a vast landscape or a first embrace.

Tiferet is the essence of Time. For man it is the cycle of the Sun through a day and night. For a mayfly, a creature whose existence is but a few hours, a day is a whole life. To the biosphere a year, the complete round of seasons, is maybe a day. To the Earth, a day is perhaps many decades, one rotation on its own axis merely being its shortest registerable impression. For the Sun, the radiation ebb and flow as measured in the Earth's tropical to ice-age cycle may be just

*Figure 47—PORTRAIT*
*A photograph catches but a moment in someone's life. It is only an image of that person at that point in life. A painting by a great artist like Rembrandt is quite different. It is the result of hundreds of glimpses, by the painter, of the person's body and soul. The mind is more penetrating than any camera, in that it can perceive the state and character of the psyche. While the garments and posture of a sitter indicate what persona they might wish to represent, a great painter can not only reveal what is hidden but the quality of the life lived. (Jacob Tripp* by Rembrandt, 17th century).

a breath. Tiferet is the slide plate of our cosmic microscope and whatever we put there, in this particular examination, will be the day and night for that entity. For us, we can see quite plainly that we live by the beat of activity and rest. One twenty-four-hour cycle is a mirror of our life. Our awakening is birth, our morning growth, noon is prime, afternoon our wane and evening our retirement with death's stepbrother, sleep, completing the circle. True, not all our dawns coincide with the clock on the wall; some of us begin to wake up at midday and others after midnight. Everyone has his or her own setting or personal chronology for the day but, without exception, everybody has to obey the ebb and flow of the cycle. The vital forces can be drawn upon to extend their period but to drain these emergency reservoirs is eventually to court death, for it is contrary to the mainspring of life which drives our personal clock.

Gevurah is a single life. In man it is connected with the emotional aspect of his being. It is the feeling of a life. Sometimes great portrait painters use this faculty to catch in their pictures the whole of a man's existence. A Rembrandt is more than a remarkable likeness. It is layer upon layer of impressions. It is the sum total of a demeanour, attitudes and deeds. In the portraits of himself he sets down his own existence, its bitterness, curiosity and love. Here are the elements that make this or that particular man different. He may be similar in many ways to a twin brother but, over a lifetime, his peculiarly personal composition shows. Gevurah is one life. For most of us it is the upper limit of a temporal appreciation. On the death of a parent the real grief is shorter than imagined. The presence of that person is soon forgotten, not out of disrespect, but in that your own life goes on. Even for the surviving spouse, providing he does not retire out of life into memories, the chances are that he will soon be considering marriage to fill up his last years. This is the sense of one life, the first and last breaths marked out by impressions and seen through the screen of Yesod. The later years fly by as the once freshly tuned organism slows down and the ageing mechanism of the body seems to dull the senses and blur the interior rhythms. However, Gevurah belongs to the company of Tiferet and Hesed, the triad of self-consciousness, and as the years accumulate so should the awareness of the non-physical realm and its other-world time. Gevurah and Hesed are the angels guarding the gates of Eden. It is possible to enter Paradise even during the sojourn in the world of action and matter. In this way man is unique and different from the animals, in that on reaching his prime he can rise

162

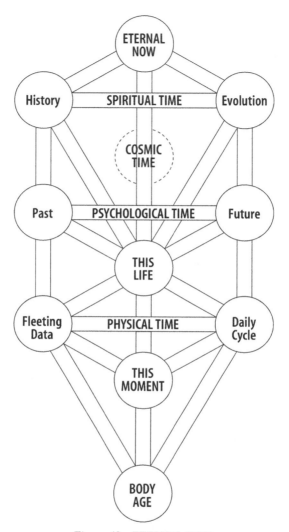

*Figure 48—ETERNAL NOW*

All that happens is against a background of total stillness. This is the Time of the Absolute. This motionless moment encompasses the various grades of Time and yet within each level it is possible to gain access to Eternity. Many kabbalistic meditations are designed to pierce through the 'Passing show' and so perceive different dimensions of Time. These include the past, which relates to the left pillar as crystallised structure while the dynamic pillar on the right indicates the potential yet to come into being. The central column is concerned with the consciousness of Time by anyone in a clear psychological or spiritual mystical state. At the bottom is the phenomenon of ordinary perception. (Halevi).

above the law of his body and carry on growing. Here he moves out of the physical laws of accident, into those of fate. If he can ascend higher up the central column he comes consciously under the hand of Destiny.

Hesed is the expansion of Time, in contrast to the contraction and differentiation of Time in Gevurah. In this sefirah it is the power that extends beyond the life of an individual. In physical terms it is the life span of the species of a creature. In this sefirah are all men, at every age and time. Here is the dynamic behind a population explosion with millions upon millions inheriting the Earth. Hesed is the great impulse of the human race spreading out over the planet from its primal origins. It is a vast scale of time. For us, we see it in the lives of previous generations, their achievements and work speaking of the human genius. Anyone who participates in this level of Time is in the least a historian, at most a great teacher founding a civilisation. This is the dimension of which we catch a glimpse when we see the Acropolis or the pyramids and more, it is the sense of countless lives all forming one being known as Man or, in kabbalistic terms, Adam.

Daat, as is to be guessed, is unique. It occupies, on the central axis of consciousness, a special place. While the sefirot of the outer columns define functions, the central ones appertain to that creature's awareness. In Yesod is the mirror image of passing time made up of the input from the other sefirot. This is a variable picture of Malkhut, when looking down. When Tiferet is the focus as the Watcher or observer (sometimes manifest, as said, in crises or accidents), Yesod becomes the obedient executive. Then Time ceases just to pass by and the person becomes, according to the need of Tiferet, attentive at the most useful level—in the case of an accident—in Nezah and Hod. With the added and cultivated facilities of Gevurah and Hesed, another dimension of Time is accessible. This is Daat, the door into Timelessness, as it allows the flow upward into Keter. This phenomenon is not the same as those memories of periods 'out of time', often felt in love affairs, but closer to profound religious experience upon which no clock, be it the 'now' of Hod or the cycle of Nezah, can be placed. Not even the glimpse of a life-time or the faint after-image of a distant epoch can be set in the same class. Daat is the edge of where Time does not exist.

Binah, in physical terms, is Nature. Included in its timescale are all the living things of organic life. It dates from the first living molecular cell and terminates with the final breath of the last dying creature on

*Figure 49—VISIONS*
*Some psychics can key into the Astral World and even converse with the discarnate. This, however, is not recommended as such encounters can lead to disturbing experiences. Kabbalists, after much training, can enter Higher Worlds because they can handle the powerful forces found there. Here a scholar opens a door into another reality but can he contain whatever entity might appear and seek to control him?* (Rembrandt etching, 17th century).

our planet. It is, to us, this side of eternity. Still within grasp of understanding, we may grope with the problems of survival common to all living things. Our museums are full of bones and shells of long-dead beings so primitive that we are revolted by the violence in which they lived and died but we can, at least, appreciate the primitive desires of the prehistoric trilobite and dinosaur. We can look across a vast gap in time and view the various organic experiments, see the evolution of plants, insects, and animals. Even now, we can recognise a twenty-million-year-old footstep on a rock and trace ferns in coal; but when we come to stone without the sign of life we stumble into another kind of time. Binah is Mother Nature, the receptacle of the creative impulse. She is the builder of prototypes, the designer of creatures and plants that are needed to clothe the Earth for a particular period. At the beginning, only simple organisms were needed to convert the incoming cosmic energy flow. Later, the planet required more sensitive receptors and Nature responded, eventually producing the body of man which could be inhabited by something more than vital force. Here was a new element added to the intelligence of the planet. Binah setting each one of her children to do a task, and working through the determinates of Gevurah below, made sure the plants and animals lived their lives within definite limits of their species. Only man could free himself from her absolute rule. That could only be achieved one life at a time, out of the general law of the species, through Daat. For a man the triad Binah-Hokhmah-Tiferet is his destiny—with the knowledge of Daat he can open a door on to the Divine and escape the Wheel of Existence.

The time of Hokhmah on this scale is the planet. For a man it is far beyond his time and yet he can perceive, in flashes of deep intellect, what the Earth's time measure might be like. He can work out, with clues given by rocks, samples from the Moon, the rhythms of the planets and the vast cycles of the Sun, what the Earth receives if it were conscious of itself. He can guess that, with its surrounding air and radiation belts, it at least exhibits the most primitive cell-like resemblance of a living being. That which appears to be dead and rigid is, in fact, in a high state of flux and even in osmosis exchange with space. The Earth, if it is alive, is not very old and man knows by deduction and speculation that in relation to the Milky Way the Solar system is less than middle-aged. On these timescales nothing has any personal meaning to man, any more than the truth that the remote galaxy of Andromeda seen today by us is, in fact, what it looked like several million years ago. These vast distances and times are only measurable in their own terms. The Sun to a man is eternal but it is no more than a flicker to the Milky Way. The planet is, for man, the Hokhmah of his Time, the progenitor of Nature and his species. It is not, however long its immense life, Eternity though in the relative world it may take on that name for an undeveloped man. Herein lies the strangeness of Time. A highly developed spiritual man may transfer himself into the next World, thereby side-stepping the usual hierarchy of age. He may, as has been said in many religions, be seen after physical death and, in some cases, return to Earth in a time or period of his own choosing. This is only possible if he has risen up the column of consciousness, a unique and rare accomplishment among millions of human existences.

Keter is the Crown. In its hollow circlet is timelessness. Beyond and above is not even timelessness. From this sefirah issues that which is manifest as Time. Time is movement. Behind movement is stillness. Behind stillness, Nothing. Keter is the Crown, gateway out of the prison even of Eternity.

In relation to the four Worlds each Tree and sefirah has its own Time, though to the lower Worlds it will seem incommensurable, the upper World being no more than a presence or possibility, like our view of life before birth or after death. It is impossible to explain our world's time in terms of another but this does not preclude experience of the miraculous when the upper realms manifest on our level of existence.

# *16. Evolution*

The Lightning Flash that zigzags down from the Crown of the Tree of Life is the descending process of Creation. There is also a reciprocal ascent from Malkhut, the Kingdom, at the bottom which is the impulse of evolution. This is the reflection of all that has been called forth, created, formed and made. Put as a conscious act of Creation, the root of this idea arises from the Holy Names of I AM That I AM. The first statement brings into being the manifestation of the Divine. The word 'That' is 'Existence' and the second 'I AM' is God beholding God in the mirror of the universe. Evolution is the development of perception through the various levels, from the densest of metals and minerals to the highest degree a human being can attain, becoming SELF- realised as the most perfect microcosmic image of the Deity.

The so-called Big Bang by which the physical world of matter and energy came into being was in fact, from a cosmic viewpoint, the initial moment of radiation of pure Divine Light. This expanded into a void which had been generated by the Holy One for Existence to appear within. This fiery emanation expanded and cooled into gas and then fluids and solids, as the ideas and then the forms of matter took on the four states of the material substances. Over time these coalesced, in the physical realm, into the form of radiant fields, cycles and frequencies that became galactic, stellar and planetary systems.

Over time our Sun became what Kabbalah calls an archangel, with the planets as angels. The Solar system, working through an evolutionary progression, then produced a situation in which organic life could exist. After the Earth had developed a core of metals and minerals, the oceans, atmosphere and electromagnetic field came into a particular state, so as to protect the delicate membrane of Nature that was to emerge once a stable weather system was in place. This occurred in the Yesod, or Foundation, of the Earth's Tree. Here semi-mineral viruses gave birth to the lowest plants which, in time, gave rise to higher plants. These could respond to various stimuli, such as sunlight, and absorb the mineral content of the water in which they lived. From them different organic species developed to meet a wide

*Figure 50—CREATION*

The Seven Days of Creation in Genesis is an allegorical version of the octave coming down the Tree of Creation. These images describe the process of increasing differentiation from pre-Light to the lowest of creatures. As yet, these beings are only essences or ideas in the World of the Spirit. However, in order to describe the indescribable, mystics often use poetic language so as to convey a sense of another reality. In this case, the Birds of the Air define the Archangels while the Fish of the Sea represent the angels. So here we see the Creation of the four elements and their inhabitants, the last being that of Earthly creatures, but still in spiritual mode. (Rev. Bank's Bible, 19th century).

variety of conditions as plants spread throughout the oceans and eventually onto the land.

Plant-animals, at stage four on the Tree, emerged as a higher order of life. They were more sophisticated in their food and modes of reproduction. Their level of consciousness was primitive but very sensitive to the immediate environment leading, in time, to the appearance of the lowest order of animals that could move freely within a limited habitat. These creatures could react more intelligently than any plant and take wider action to obtain nourishment. Their mobility allowed them, moreover, to breed over a larger area of sea and invade the land. These invertebrates like insects learned to swim, crawl and fly. Such a capacity allowed them to exploit the planet. They were, for a very long time, the highest form of life on the Earth.

Then came the long epoch of the fish and reptiles with spines and small but well-organised nervous systems. These fleshy beings could reflect, to a degree, upon their local conditions and adapt to what suited them. This gave rise to increasing differentiation. Out of this arose the first mammals which could survive in climates that reptiles could not tolerate. Thus they became the most advanced organic beings on Earth.

Of these, the primates reached a point of development in which they acquired primitive thought based upon experience and insight. These apes were to be the physical vehicle by which human beings could descend from what is called the Treasure House of Souls. Humans, in essence, according to Kabbalah, are not creatures but have their origin in the Divine realm of Adam Kadmon, the image of God in the highest World of Emanation. Each spark of human consciousness is a part of the anatomy of this primordial reflection of the Godhead. It was when the 'second', spiritual Adam, who was both male and female, emerged on the Sixth Day of Creation that mankind began to descend, in order to fulfill the Absolute's plan to behold 'ITSELF' through human perception. In the World of Creation, humanity became enclothed in Spirit before the next lower stage of being separated out into male and female souls in the Garden of Eden.

It was in Paradise, the realm between Heaven and Earth, that the two aspects of humanity, symbolised by the Biblical Adam and Eve, were enclothed in a form that corresponds to the psyche. Here the couple spent some time getting used to existing in what some call the Astral plane. However, the Garden of Eden was so pleasant that the Holy One had to have a contingency plan to get humanity out of it and

*Figure 51—SYMBOLISM*
*It is said that the Bible can be understood in four ways. The lowest is the literal, in*
*which events are taken at their face value. The second is allegorical which speaks to*
*the soul in metaphor. The third is metaphysical that explains in concepts, diagrams*
*and geometry the Laws of Existence. The highest is direct mystical experience of the*
*Divine. In this image of Paradise are the forms of Nature in their perfection. In the*
*Garden is the Tree of Knowledge, representing the World of Creation, while above is*
*the Divine Tree of Life. The material universe is yet to be created, formed and made.*
(Medieval woodcut).

down to the lowest realm of Earthly materiality in order to carry out their mission to be the organs of perception for God. Adam and Eve, the archetypes of the human race, were told that they were not to eat of the Tree of Knowledge, knowing full well they would be tempted by Satan the Tester. Having eaten of the forbidden fruit, Adam and Eve became Self-conscious and therefore had access to Higher Knowledge which they could not, as yet, handle because they were so far without experience. In order to avoid them partaking of the Divine Tree of Life above, and so wield Divine power, they were told they were to be sent down to the level of Earth because they had 'sinned'. In Hebrew the word means 'miss the mark'. This is not quite so damning as conventional religion would have us believe. It was the first lesson about karma.

So it was that humanity had to put on 'coats of skin', in other words, be incarnated into the natural and elemental habitat. The subtle body of the psyche is designed to integrate with an organic vehicle. Evidence indicates that, some three to five million years ago in Africa, two infants were born that were quite different from other primates. This was not unusual in the evolutionary scheme of things. This embodied pair soon recognised what they had in common when they mated and split off from their ape clan. This was an established primate custom, to start a family line of their own.

Over time the human clan increased and spread all over the world, living almost like animals but not quite. They were inventive and imaginative so that they could exploit their environment to the maximum. Apes had simple tools but they never produced a flint scraping knife or bow and arrow. What is more, human reflection went beyond the immediate. They considered the past and future, the sky, birth and death. No other creature on Earth had ever considered the pattern of the seasons, the crucial positions of the Sun and Moon or the precise time to plant. This observation brought about the agricultural revolution and the domestication of animals.

Such developments were the result of both collective and individual effort. A person would discover a new technique, or exploit an inspired idea, which would then become a part of that tribe's culture. As basic needs were met, it gave time for some individuals to develop. Some used their greater skills to dominate their fellows while others applied their increased intelligence to ponder Existence and raise the level of their community. These people became the shamans and priests while the shrewd turned into the leaders of the tribe. Here to

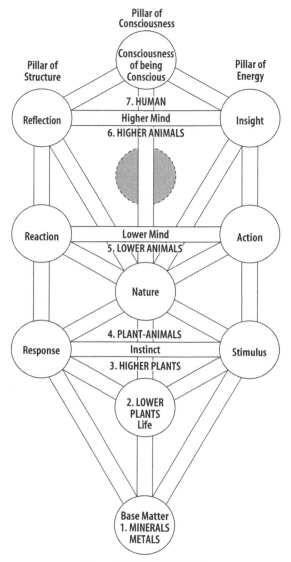

*Figure 52—EVOLUTION*
*Here the descending impulse, having reached the lowest sefirah of the Tree of*
*Materiality, now turns upward towards its Source. Slowly, different phases of life*
*emerge, composed of the four elements but organic in their make-up as they evolve*
*through ascending stages. Human beings came down from the Garden of Eden when*
*there was a body advanced enough to be the vehicle that the human psyche and spirit*
*could inhabit. This body contained all the other levels of evolution. (Halevi).*

be seen is the vegetable, animal and human hierarchy that was to emerge within the level of barbarity and, later, civilisation.

The vegetable level of survival is largely made up of the young souls who had descended from Eden later than their older and more experienced leaders who themselves had been reincarnated many times in the process called, in Kabbalah, the *Gilgulim* or cycle of life and death. The notion of reincarnation is common to both primitive and advanced cultures. In the Jewish esoteric tradition, the concept of transmigration of souls from one body to another and over the generations is accepted. It was part of the early Church's belief until it was voted a heresy by a priesthood that was more interested in conformity than spirituality.

Evolution is seen in a shift from the simple savage states of nomadic clans to the barbaric level of tribes that also traded with each other, as well as making war. This economic factor gave rise to cities on trade routes. These centres began to attract master merchants, artisans and an intelligentsia. This focus of wealth and culture attracted individuals who no longer wished to live the hard life of the wilderness and farm. Towns also offered these awakening souls new opportunities and a freedom from tribal custom. Out of an atmosphere of enterprise arose the high arts, the beginning of science and a judiciary and philosophy to balance the superstitious aspect of religion.

The idea of Law and Justice arose from the most advanced souls who saw that a nation or civilisation could not survive, let alone progress, without a code of morality. This came initially from the visions of prophets, those who cultivated reason, and the mystics who, by now, were certain that the invisible realms were governed by cosmic and moral principles that came from an unknown Absolute. The priests who served in the temples to some god, who represented one of the celestial bodies or great nature spirits, founded the first universities that studied all the collected knowledge of their culture. However, in some sacred places there were schools of the soul that were concerned with esoteric matters.

These usually discreet institutions were for those who wished to develop themselves consciously, as against evolving slowly over many lifetimes. Such individuals had usually reached a critical point of sensitivity. On their own, such people could only go so far. They needed help, as it was very easy to become deluded about what they saw and experienced in clear moments during private meditation or contemplation of life and the universe. Here is where the old souls who had attained a degree of enlightenment taught the doctrine of the micro- and macrocosm, their purpose and relation to the ultimate Deity.

# 17. Schools of the Soul

Schools of the soul may be found in the heart of a great city or in a remote desert, if there is a need for them to be there. Some monasteries of the Dark Ages in Europe were esoteric schools, as were meetings of what were called the 'Elders' in the African bush. Gatherings in private houses of ancient Alexandria, conclaves in royal courts and the study rooms of synagogues were the places where Higher Knowledge was discussed. Most had lay tutors while some had master teachers. All had a theoretical system and practical exercises and, most important, a discipline. A school might exist for a generation or three hundred years. After they had fulfilled their function, sometimes only the shell of a school, in the form of a religious or philosophical sect, was left. Occasionally, a distortion of the Teaching was claimed by a 'Dark Teacher' who convinced their followers that only they possessed such knowledge. These conditions are still in operation today, so that the seeker must test and double-check that what is on offer is genuine.

The structure of an esoteric school is universal as it follows the Divine pattern set out on the Tree. It may be a very simple situation, with a few committed people meeting in someone's home, or it might be composed of hundreds of students stretching around the world. All, however, need—as the Tree indicates—a place to meet. In Biblical times the Temple in Jerusalem had its discreet chambers where a cabal of priests and rabbis would meet. Down by the Dead Sea, a cave might perform the same rôle. In the medieval times a room above a tavern in Toledo was a meeting place for Jews, Christians and Moslems who shared the same love for Truth and Higher Knowledge. In modern times it could be a New York apartment or a back room in the university of Oxford. Meetings have been known to take place in a forest glade, an ancient ruin or even in the office of a government building. The most well known venue is the Masonic Lodge.

The teacher should be a man or woman who is mature and has been through a long training in psychology and cosmology. He or she must

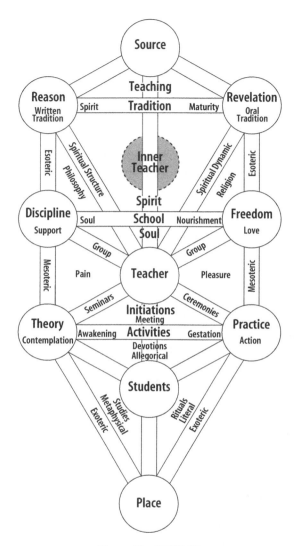

*Figure 53—SCHOOL*
*Here is the organisation of a school of the soul. The teacher can be of any tradition*
*but their relationship with their students is essentially the same, as are the working*
*methods. The meetings, seminars or ceremonies are where initiations occur, in that*
*realisations happen at such gatherings. A school is usually within a general tradition.*
*The triads of pain and pleasure are about what has to be given up and what is gained.*
*This leads to a more profound comprehension of the Teaching. The spirit of the*
*School is often the original founder, who may have died centuries before, working*
*through whoever is incarnate at the centre of the Tree.* (Halevi).

be well acquainted with his tradition as it relates to his place and time. He must understand the local culture so as to be able to convey the Teaching very clearly and speak from his own inner experience of the higher Worlds, otherwise it is but words. A tutor must be kind and wise but firm when needed, also have a sense of humour and be a good story-teller to make symbols and concepts come alive. All the great masters had the ability to illuminate a student with a parable or joke.

Students may be drawn from all walks of life and from both sexes. They may come for different reasons and levels but all usually wish to know what life and the universe is really about. Thus the uneducated artisan may be further along the Path than the academic professor who can only quote while a housewife may be more perceptive than a worldly-wise businessman. Some students have found their school after a long search. It takes time to find the one that suits their temperament. In contrast, someone else may recognise the hint of a school dropped in a seemingly casual conversation. Needless to say, not all who join a school stay. The reason for leaving may be because it is too much commitment to take on or not profound enough for them. It could be the end of a fantasy that fades when serious inner work to develop is required. Some leave because they believe they know more than the teacher or it can be the time is not yet right for them because they have to learn more about life.

The theory and practices are seen in the Ways of Action, Devotion and Contemplation. These may take the form of rituals, meditation and studies. Each school has its own form which may or may not relate to everyone's needs. This is partly dependent upon the character of the teacher, who will be inclined to be a doer, feeler or thinker. There is also the astrological factor. A Scorpio instructor will attract Water and Earth signs, whereas a Leo would draw Airy and Fiery people. Usually there is a mixture if the teacher has an Earthy Sun and Airy Moon or a Watery Moon and Fiery Sun. The methods applied by the teacher will give the school a certain mode which will be related to the particular purpose for which it was brought into being.

An example of this is the Freemasons whose movement was founded during the period of religious conflict between Catholics and Protestants. People of goodwill, on both sides, needed a neutral meeting place. Based upon the idea of Solomon's Temple and the medieval guild of cathedral builders, individuals seeking knowledge of the higher Worlds could gather in what was called a Lodge to study and

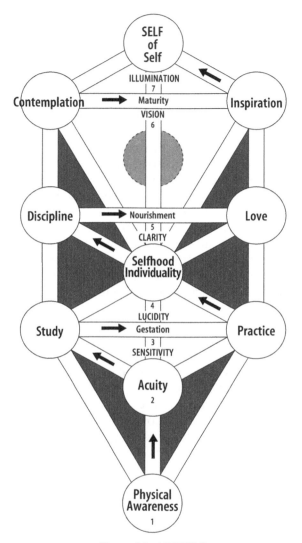

*Figure 54—METHOD*

*These are the seven levels of the psyche which give access to the seven upper Halls of the spirit. The ascent is via the side pillars on the upward movement of the Lightning Flash. At the bottom is simple instinctive awareness, then comes a sensitivity to social activity followed by a psychic ability. Above this feeling level comes an animal-like sharpness in lucidity with the soul triad acquiring a clarity that can perceive a whole life. Beyond this personal level is vision, or a transpersonal and spiritual perception of reality. At the top comes illumination, where the individual Self encounters the Divine SELF of the Self. This place is where the three upper Worlds meet. (Halevi).*

practise esoteric principles. This function relates to the triad of initiations. Such gatherings might be once a week, month or certain times of year. Here is where the lower psyche gestates prior to the birth of the soul.

The pain and pleasure triads are about profound changes within the student's being. Some are delightful, as experience enlarges the person's horizon, while some suffering can come from recognising and discarding useless attitudes, habits and the shadow side of the psyche. Pleasure may manifest in good and true company while pain might come in ending a love relationship with someone not interested in development. This process of purification and balance is continuous. The sefirot of discipline and freedom nourish the soul which begins to emerge from the unconscious as the Self of Tiferet takes over from the dominance of the Yesodic ego. The Dark Night of the Soul, spoken of in various traditions, is about the process of shaking off the shackles of the super-ego ideal that imprisons people within their family, class or collective tribal conditioning. To be a true individual requires courage and integrity. Consider those who have stood up to tyranny or the disapproval of their family in order to be true to themselves. Here is where the support of a school of the soul is vital.

Most schools belong to a tradition. In this case it is the kabbalistic line of the Judaeo-Christian civilisation of the West. Since its inception with Abraham, it has adjusted in every period so that its Teaching is up to date. In Biblical times the mode was history and symbolism. Indeed, it was said that the Bible contained four levels, each one corresponding to one of the Worlds. The literal understanding of the text was related to the realm of Action; the allegorical to that of Formation, where archetypes such as Adam and Eve reside. The metaphysical is paralleled with the spiritual realm of Creation while the mystical appertains to the Divine and highest World. In the Middle Ages, Neo-Platonism was the language of philosophy, then the intellectual fashion of the time. This was adopted by the Jewish mystics to solve the problem of which truth was superior, religious revelation or philosophical speculation. Out of this conflict, what became known as the kabbalistic tradition was born.

The inner teacher, seen in the position of Daat, is usually the founder of a particular line. In Kabbalah, it might be the 11th century Spanish poet and philosopher, Solomon Ibn Gabirol, whose spirit might reside over a particular school. Conversely, in the Christian tradition, it could be St. Theresa of Avila who founded an important

180

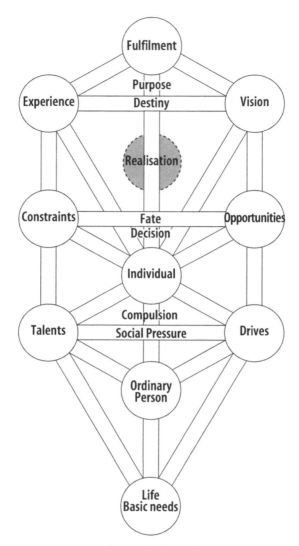

*Figure 55 — WORK*
In Kabbalah, there is no retreat from the outside world. Indeed, the aim is to operate in the marketplace where there is the maximum possibility to develop amid the hurly-burly of life. As one rabbi observed, 'One can learn even from a thief, as they are always alert'. Thus a life under esoteric discipline utilises talents and drives to fulfil its potential. Over time, a person knows what to avoid and what to exploit in order to evolve and make use of their fate. Then, with long experience of perhaps many lives, an individual can recognise what their destiny is and so play a conscious part in Existence's purpose. (Halevi).

school in the 16th century. Many Sufis follow the example of Ibn Arabi even though some Moslems see him as a heretic. This is inevitable when any tradition becomes a formal and rigid religion or philosophy and sees anything contrary to its ideology as a threat. The intelligent and beautiful scholar and teacher, Hypatia of Alexandria, was murdered by a mob because her mystical philosophy at the university attracted too many Christians. Her spirit lives, however, as an ideal for many women aspiring to develop.

In the topmost triad is the eternal Teaching which is at the core of every genuine esoteric tradition. Reason and Revelation, moreover, are not confined to the sophisticated. It is to be found in the inner teachings of so-called Native peoples. An esoteric master might be a stall trader in some village market or a carpenter. The great Plotinus' tutor was a port docker. One rabbi discovered after his teacher's death that he had been a merchant. Sometimes a master has to adopt a misleading persona in order to protect himself and his school from hostile orthodox authorities.

The seven levels up the centre of the Tree define degrees of the psyche and internal development. It begins with making one's physical awareness more sharp. This is why many traditions use ritual to enhance the senses and the body's inner and outer state. In Kabbalah there are certain exercises, like walking while holding the two side pillars of the Tree in balance in relation to the central column of the body. Any activity, be it mundane or social, may be used to raise one's level. In the synagogue, those saying their prayers may be seen swaying backwards and forwards. This motion represents the flame of the Divine within, while the hands of a Christian or Moslem worshipper are clasped together or opened out to signify focused attention and receive Grace respectively. Most people are oblivious of the profound purpose of such symbols.

The state of acuity is to be to be sharply aware of the general situation around one and to be keenly observant of everyday matters. There is a lesson to be learned in every situation if one is watchful. The triad of sensitivity is about the psychic capacity of the lower psyche. This can pick up what the senses cannot detect, such as a certain tension or mood which body language does not reveal. This is most useful when relating to people who conceal what they really feel. Lucidity is to make use of the animal instinct to see the dynamics of an event and exploit, in a positive way, what may be learned about one's own and others' motivation. This is vital in esoteric work as misinformation or passion can disrupt one's studies or divert attention. 'Know thyself' was an ancient dictum and one must never ignore the power of the instincts and mental conditioning that can prevent personal evolution.

The soul triad is awakened when the individual makes the Self the centre of gravity within their being. Then a clarity about the whole of their life comes into focus. They can see objectively, to a degree, what their fate is about and know what to do after Gevurah and Hesed have considered the issue. A helpful kabbalistic maxim is, 'If in doubt, do the right thing'. This piece of advice is based upon the fact that the soul is the moral arbiter of the psyche. The lower face is too greatly influenced by practical considerations while the upper face is too transpersonal to take the immediate question into account. The great triad of the Spirit is primarily concerned with cosmic matters. The soul is the zone of free will. Below, wilfulness is pressure from the right-hand pillar and will-lessness can occur when the left-hand pillar is dominant. The feeling triad on the central column can stimulate willingness and help the lucid triad to develop a true willpower. This, however, being animal by nature, has to be obedient to the Self and soul.

When the will of the Self is submitted to God, then the great spiritual triad opens up to a wider vision. In this one's destiny is seen and how it fits into the general process of human evolution, as each one of us can contribute much to history in some small or large way. While some people may become well known there are many who, unseen or unnoticed, greatly influence others just by their radiant presence or sane opinion. For example, a lady kabbalist always stopped people being grossly vulgar by just entering the office where she worked; while a wise piece of advice to a public figure based upon kabbalistic principles turned a crucial speech into a profound political statement. Indeed, the great creative movements in history have usually been brought about by a discreet effort of someone in a school of the soul. Isaac Newton was a Freemason who changed the direction of science.

Maturity comes when contemplation and inspiration come together. Such a situation may well precipitate illumination. This may not be of the order of Buddha but it can change the life of that individual and others who might come in contact with them. Such an event is usually arranged by Providence for just the right moment when the people involved are receptive and understand what they are being shown. This often occurs in a crisis situation but it can happen in a moment of great peace that can fatally alter many lives.

There is a kabbalistic tradition that there are thirty-six hidden saints and sages whose mission it is to be where they are needed at the right moment. In reality, there is a whole hierarchy of advanced souls, some in the flesh and others who are discarnate, who watch over particular individuals and situations that need monitoring. They will not interfere with people's free will but can aid those who are receptive to hints or omens which indicate that transformation is imminent if they want it. These guides can also intervene when protection is required on the transpersonal scale. An example is George Washington who escaped unharmed despite having his coat shot through and horses killed under him. This is the work of the hidden 'watchers', as they are called, who may be incarnate or discarnate humans who are no longer subject to karma and live accordingly to the laws of the higher Worlds.

184

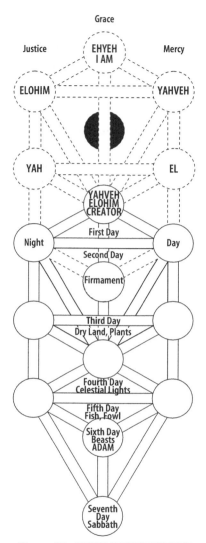

*Figure 56—INTERCONNECTIONS*

*Here, in Tree terms, can be seen how the second and separate World of Creation emerges from the Divine realm. It begins at the centre of the upper Tree of Emanation where the Creator brings forth the spiritual universe. From here the Seven Days unfold. Upon completion, we see that what is called the upper face of Creation overlays the lower face of the Divine Tree. Thus they may relate, even though they are separate. This process of separation and interaction is seen in the two lower Worlds of Formation and Action. Thus the body and psyche are able to work together from birth to death. (Halevi).*

# 18. Jacob's Ladder

Up to this point we have been only looking at the single Tree, viewing it from many angles, in order to see how it is the basis of all organised activity in the universe. In one chapter we saw how the idea of four Worlds was inherent in the structure of the original Divine Tree of Emanation. These four levels, manifested in various modes such as Fire, Air, Water and Earth, can be seen in the human body as the conscious, electronic, chemical and mechanical principles. We will now introduce the kabbalistic concept of Jacob's Ladder or the extended Tree.

We began with the origin of the primordial Tree, the realm of the potential. Now comes the actualisation through the emergence of the spiritual Tree of Creation. The process begins at the Tiferet of the Tree of Azilut where the Holy Names, YAHVEH and ELOHIM, combine to become the CREATOR. Prompted by I AM beyond the Daat or veil above, the Will of the Absolute initiates Creation. This is described in the first chapter of Genesis in a symbolic form. However, the metaphysics of the Seven Days is very precise when seen kabbalistically.

First, Light is separated from Darkness. This indicates that the singularity of the Crown of Creation is transformed into a trinity with the Will of God at the head of what will become the three pillars. Then comes the division of the Firmament, that is, Fire is separated from Air or the Divine from the Spirit, followed by the differentiation of Water and Earth. These elements are still, it must again be said, not physical but spiritual concepts of Matter. They, in turn, on the Fourth Day are organised into a well-ordered Cosmos and time frame. Into this World of Ideas now come the Birds of the Air and the Fish of the Sea. These represent the archangels and angels that will inhabit the Airy and Watery dimensions of Creation and Formation. On the Sixth Day the Beasts of the Field are created. These represent the creatures that will eventually incarnate in the physical universe. Finally the second 'spiritual Adam', both male and female, emerges just before the Octave of Creation comes to an end.

From the Tiferet of Creation, which is also the Malkhut of the

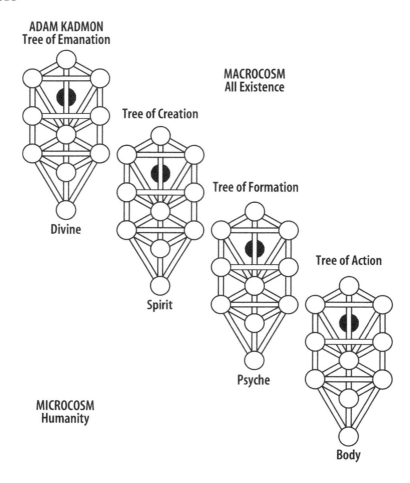

*Figure 57—FOUR WORLDS*
When the process of bringing Existence into being is complete, there are four separate but interconnected realities at the macrocosmic level. In the microcosm of a human being, these Worlds can be seen as the body, psyche, spirit and Divine. Kabbalah gives a detailed account of each World in symbolic and metaphysical terms. Both concur with the idea of the Chain of Being common to all esoteric lines. Some traditions regard the lower levels of Existence as inferior, and even evil, but Kabbalah sees the whole of Existence as a Divine expression, so that even evil has its function to test the good and destroy the bad. Without death and destruction the universe could never renew itself. (Halevi).

Divine, the fluidic World of Formation then begins to emerge. This means that the Keter or Crown of Formation is in direct contact with the two higher realms. This is crucial in the plan of Evolution, as it means that it is possible to cross three zones and gain access to the highest Worlds from below. This is vital in the case of humanity as the means by which the Absolute views every level of Existence through every human experience.

The World of Formation is the Garden of Eden. However, the so-called upper and lower faces of its Tree divide into a Heavenly and an Earthly Paradise. This is because the higher part overlaps the lower face of Creation while the lower part of Eden overlays the upper face of the physical World when it comes into being. This astral World is not only the Treasure House of Souls, from which all humans will descend and return to in the life and death cycle of *Gilgulim*, but the site of Hell. This is at the very bottom of the Astral realm where evil people spend time between lives facing their misdemeanours. Like Heaven, there are said to be seven levels. The lowest is often defined in elemental terms of fire, blasting winds, freezing ice and crushing earth. These symbols represent psychic states of afflicted souls.

The upper part of Paradise is the domain of the celestial universities. Here, evolved souls meet and develop after death, before the next life. This is the place where discarnate teachers in every field are to be found, along with all the great works of mankind that have been lost and no longer exist on Earth. The various myths and legends of an idyllic world have their roots in mystics' visions of such a place. The kabbalistic version of this *Shangri La* is called the *Yeshivot on High* where the most evolved saints and sages teach the more advanced souls. Below, the Earthly Paradise is a perfect image of the natural world beneath. It has the best of weather and terrain where families and soul groups can meet in the afterlife. Here they rest and reflect upon their performance, as well as enjoy each other's company before being reborn.

The lowest World of Materiality emerges out of the place where the three lower Worlds meet. Here is where the Big Bang began. From this burst of emanation from Creation via Formation, the four states of matter, in physical substance, came into Existence. This is where the return journey of evolution, described in an earlier chapter, begins. At the head of the seventh level of the Earthly Tree is humanity.

As said, human beings have donned a physical body for the purpose of being the organ of perception for the Absolute. However, they have

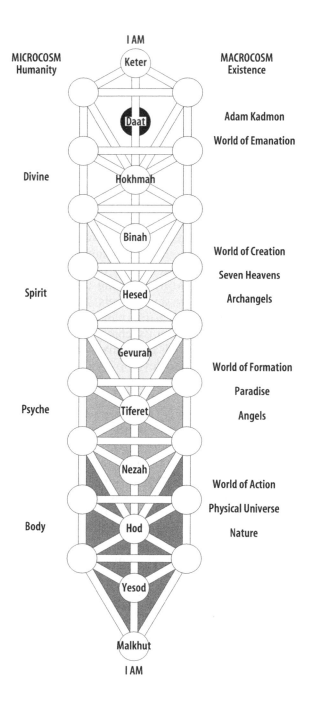

I AM

MICROCOSM
Humanity

MACROCOSM
Existence

Keter

Adam Kadmon

Daat

World of Emanation

Divine

Hokhmah

Binah

World of Creation

Seven Heavens

Spirit

Hesed

Archangels

Gevurah

World of Formation

Paradise

Psyche

Tiferet

Angels

Nezah

World of Action

Physical Universe

Body

Hod

Nature

Yesod

Malkhut

I AM

to learn how to be such an instrument both at the personal and collective levels. It has taken several million years to reach the present point of consciousness, as individuals and *en masse*. This is seen in the wide spectrum of cultures from the most primitive to the most advanced. The grades can be seen clearly in every city, where the criminal element corresponds to the savage level while great saints and sages go about their work of assisting others to develop at every social level.

The completion of the four Worlds brought about a new dimension. This was of a fifth Tree that locked them all together, making what is called the *Kav* link of Divine Grace and Presence throughout Existence. In this way the Holy One can intervene, if needed, by applying the power of a higher World to a lower. Such remarkable events are called miracles. The parting of the Red Sea for the Israelites is an example of wind pressure being adjusted to blow the waters apart. So it is in with many people that miraculous and providential coincidences change their lives.

With Jacob's Ladder, the full picture of Existence can be seen. From a macrocosmic angle one can perceive how the Worlds interlock and interact. Thus for example, the planets, which are but the bodies of great astral beings, can be seen as crucial influences upon the Earth, general evolution and human history. What made millions of people migrate from Europe to America, Africa and Australia? Each person, no doubt, had their own reason but it was, in reality, the mood of the time that caused most to uproot from home and begin a new life in often very difficult conditions. Around the year 1848 there were many revolutions due, it is said, to Uranus and Saturn. The principles of radicalism and conservatism conjoining in Aries along with Pluto, the archetype of death and transformation. Such a combination would generate revolt against any restricting political establishment.

On the microcosmic scale the four Worlds may be seen as four levels within a human being. These are the physical, psychological, spiritual

---

*Figure 58—THE GREAT TREE*

*When all four Trees are integrated a fifth Great Tree emerges. This enables the Divine to observe and intervene, if needed, at any level. I AM is in the stone as well as in a man or angelic being. The four Worlds, each with ten sefirot, make up the recurring number of forty which signifies a complete process. This is symbolised in the forty years or days mentioned in the Bible. Further, the fifty gates hinted at in Kabbalah refer to all five Trees. Sometimes only forty-nine are referred to, as the Crown of Crowns is the ultimate destination related to the Absolute. As can be seen, the sefirot are here in a vertical line called the* Kav *with Daat as the veil before the Godhead. (Halevi).*

Integra Naturæ 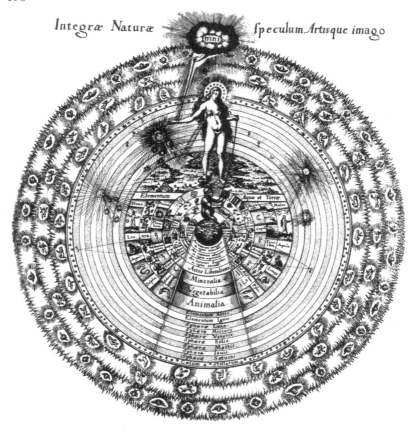 Speculum Artisque imago

*Figure 59—MIRROR*

*In this engraving, Existence is seen as but a reflection of the Absolute, here represented by the Holy and radiant Name YHVH at the top. The outermost circle corresponds to the Divine realm which contains the lower Worlds of Creation and Formation. These bring into being the physical World of stars, planets and nature. Within this innermost sphere are the levels of mineral, plant and animal with Adam and Eve representing humanity. These physical entities are made up of the four elements. The monkey represents the ordinary mind trying to understand Existence while above is the feminine symbol of the Holy Spirit. This, in another tradition, is called Sophia who holds the Worlds together.* (Robert Fludd, 17th century).

and Divine aspects that compose a person. What is done to develop the inner vehicles, as they are sometimes called, is up to the individual. As we have seen in earlier chapters, the Path up the centre of Jacob's Ladder is there to be taken. However, first one must learn to live on Earth, relate to family, friends and society before embarking upon the inner journey. It is said there are four great journeys. The first is that of descent into matter. Then comes taking part in the general evolution of mankind, before working upon one's personal development. That is the second journey of ascent, through psychological and spiritual discipline. Then upon reaching a degree of maturity comes the third journey of descent, through reincarnation, to aid others who consciously wish to evolve. This third operation may cover centuries and many incarnations to different times and places in order to carry out a specific mission. This is quite different from the normal cycle of the transmigration of a soul in the chain of generations. Here there is some degree of choice, as there has been a degree of clearing whatever karma, good and bad, the person has incurred. Such individuals have the hallmark of knowing what their work in life is. This is their destiny. For example, a healer may be, in one period, a witch-doctor of a tribe, a physician in medieval London or a psychiatrist in modern New York. Some people can actually recall former lives in this rôle and know, even when children, exactly what their career will be.

Those who are relatively advanced become the lesser saints and sages who run esoteric schools, discreetly guide nations or advise influential individuals. Their rôles may be carried out on Earth or while they are discarnate, acting as the guiding spirit to a soul group. Such people may appear as gifted scientists, practitioners of the Arts, philosophers and even priests, taking evolution on by discovery and the refinement of new ideas and forms that can take human society on a stage further.

Destruction is the opposite pole of Creation. This is quite different from human evil. Tragic events are often the result of human greed, obsession with power and money and many other negative traits. Indifference and collusion with evil is common. Many quite ordinary people supported the Nazis, spied for the Inquisition or agreed to fight in a war without thought. Quite normally respectable people have committed terrible crimes while in military uniform, only 'obeying orders'. All these acts generated both personal and collective karma which must, sooner or later and if no remorse is felt, result in them perhaps being victims of equivalent violence in some future life. This

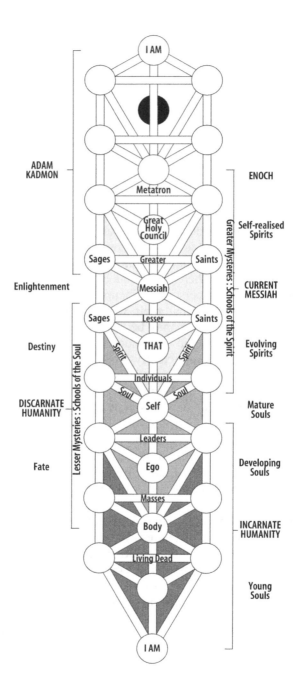

explains why so much suffering occurs and will continue until people start to develop. Like a wise parent, God has to allow the consequences of each evil action so that the sinner can learn never to do it again.

The greater saints and sages do not need to incarnate unless a new spiritual impulse is needed. The founders of great movements in history are usually very old and advanced souls who descend to meet some spiritual need. For example, between the fifth and first centuries BCE there was a wave of great teachers, such as Zoroaster, Plato and Confucius, who moved humanity on from a general barbarity to the possibility of a civilised society. Some of these teachers are, no doubt, members of what is called the Great Holy Council of fully Self-realised human spirits. Their incarnated connection on Earth is the Messiah who is fully conscious of what is going on in humanity. According to Kabbalah, King Solomon held this position as did Moses, Buddha and Jesus. The 'Anointed' is called, in the Sufi line, the 'Axis of the Age'. In India they are seen as the Maitreya. It can be a man or woman who may hold the position for a day or a lifetime, depending on what is needed at that point in history.

At the top of this hierarchy is Metatron, a human being with archangelic powers. He was Enoch, the first fully Self-realised individual. As such, he presides over the Great Holy Council as the direct representative of the Creator. He appears in history in different forms, as Time is no problem for such a being. He was Melchizedek, the priest king, who had neither father nor mother, a hint of his supernatural state. He also took on the body of Elijah but he has been known to appear as a beggar, a beautiful woman and many other guises to help saints and sages out of difficult situations.

The final and fourth journey is to climb to the top of the Ladder and directly experience the Divine. Many mystics have written about such an event. At the end of Time, the Resurrection will bring all humanity, at every level, back into the Divine realm as they return to their place

---

*Figure 60—SITUATION*
*At this point in human evolution, people of different levels are found on every rung of Jacob's Ladder. At the bottom are those who have, for this life, lost the possibility of further development. Above them come the youngest souls who tend to be dominated by animal people. Above them come those who have begun to individuate. Over the triangle of the soul are the lesser and greater saints and sages with whoever is the current Messiah. Beyond them is the Great Holy Council of Self- realised individuals, headed by Enoch, alias Metatron, the first fully developed human being and Teacher of Teachers. (Halevi).*

194

*Figure 61—COMPLETION*
At the end of Time, when humanity has developed as far as it can in this cosmic
Shemittah or cycle, the Resurrection will occur. This means the rolling-up of Jacob's
Ladder as humanity returns to Adam Kadmon. This radiant figure, seen here in the
form of the Holy Name, YHVH, presented in a vertical mode, will then become the
completed SELF-portrait of the Absolute. If it is not, then a new canvas will be called
forth, created, formed and made, so that the Godhead may experiment, as with earlier
Worlds, to find the best mode of SELF-expression. We may then, each according to
our merit, continue the process. (Calligraphy by Halevi).

within the body of Adam Kadmon from where they originally came. As all their experience is synthesised in this radiant image of the Absolute, this SELF-portrait will see that it is but a reflection, as God beholds God through all humanity's eyes. Then the whole scheme of Jacob's Ladder, and all it contains, will disappear into NO-THING-NESS again—until, perhaps, a new cycle begins.

# Index

Lightning Source UK Ltd.
Milton Keynes UK
UKOW06n1448160615

253524UK00007B/81/P